Hedda

Tanika Gupta

Inspired by Henrik Ibsen

methuen | drama

LONDON • NEW YORK • OXFORD • NEW DELHI • SYDNEY

METHUEN DRAMA
Bloomsbury Publishing Plc, 50 Bedford Square, London, WC1B 3DP, UK
Bloomsbury Publishing Inc, 1359 Broadway, New York, NY 10018, USA
Bloomsbury Publishing Ireland, 29 Earlsfort Terrace, Dublin 2,
D02 AY28, Ireland

BLOOMSBURY, METHUEN DRAMA and the Methuen
Drama logo are trademarks of Bloomsbury Publishing Plc.

First published in Great Britain 2025

Cover design: Annie Rushton

Cover photograph: Roy J Baron

Bloomsbury Publishing Plc does not have any control over, or responsibility
for, any third-party websites referred to or in this book. All internet addresses
given in this book were correct at the time of going to press. The author and
publisher regret any inconvenience caused if addresses have changed or sites
have ceased to exist, but can accept no responsibility for any such changes.

No rights in incidental music or songs contained in the work are hereby
granted and performance rights for any performance/presentation
whatsoever must be obtained from the respective copyright owners.

All rights whatsoever in this play are strictly reserved and application
for performance etc. should be made before rehearsals by professionals
and by amateurs to Casarotto Ramsay & Associates Ltd, 3rd Floor, 7 Savoy
Court, Strand, London WC2R 0EX, Mail to: agents@casarotto.co.uk.
No performance may be given unless a licence has been obtained.

A catalogue record for this book is available from the British Library.

A catalog record for this book is available from the Library of Congress.

ISBN: PB: 978-1-3505-9767-9
ePDF: 978-1-3505-9768-6
eBook: 978-1-3505-9769-3

Series: Modern Plays

Typeset by Mark Heslington Ltd, Scarborough, North Yorkshire

For product safety related questions contact
productsafety@bloomsbury.com.

To find out more about our authors and books visit
www.bloomsbury.com and sign up for our newsletters.

Hedda had its world premiere at the Orange Tree Theatre on 18 October 2025 with the following cast and creative team:

George Tesman	Joe Bannister
Alice Smith	Bebe Cave
Hedda Gabler	Pearl Chanda
Shona	Rina Fatania
Aunt Julia	Caroline Harker
Leonard	Jake Mann
John Brack	Milo Twomey

Writer	Tanika Gupta
Director	Hettie Macdonald
Set Designer	Simon Kenny
Costume Designer	Sheena Napier
Lighting Designer	Ben Ormerod
Sound Designer and Composer	Pouya Ehsaei
Casting Director	Helena Palmer CDG
Fight Director	Ruth Cooper-Brown for Rc-Annie
Assistant Director	Tara Jamora Oppen
Costume Supervisor	Cieranne Kennedy-Bell
Production Manager	Sean Laing
Deputy Stage Manager	Thomas Manly
Assistant Stage Manager	Irene Saviozzi

Special thanks go to: Lucy Briers, Shaheen Khan, Natalie Mitson, Sam Otto and Geoffrey Streatfeild.

Tanika Gupta – Writer

Previous stage credits include: *A Tupperware of Ashes*, *Sanctuary*, *The Good Woman of Setzuan*, *The Waiting Room* (National Theatre); *The Empress* (RSC, Lyric Hammersmith Theatre); *Great Expectations* (Watford Palace Theatre, Royal Exchange Theatre, ETT); *Lions and Tigers*, *A Midsummer Night's Dream* (Shakespeare's Globe); *The Overseas Student*, *A Doll's House* (Lyric Hammersmith Theatre); *Mirror on the Moor*, *Catch*, *Sugar Mummies* (Royal Court Theatre); *Red Dust Road* (Edinburgh International Festival); *A Short History of Tractors in Ukrainian* (Hull Truck); *Anita and Me*, *Love N Stuff*, *Broad* (Stratford East); *Mindwalking* (UK tour); *Dreaming by Day* (Unicorn Theatre); *2 Young 2 Luv* (Birmingham Rep); *Meet the Mukherjees* (Bolton Octagon); *Gladiator Games* (Sheffield Theatres, Stratford East); *Hobson's Choice* (Young Vic, Royal Exchange Theatre); *Fragile Land* (Hampstead Theatre).

Television credits include: *The Bill*; *Crossroads*; *All About Me*; *EastEnders*; *Grange Hill*; *London Bridge*; *Flight*; *Banglatown Banquet*.

Film credits include: *Bideshi*; *The Fiancée*; *Non-Resident*.

She has written extensively for BBC Radio 4 drama. Her play *The Empress* and her adaptation of Ibsen's *A Doll's House* are also included on the GCSE curriculum.

Tanika was awarded an MBE in 2008 for services to the arts.

Hettie Macdonald – Director

Stage directing credits include: *Sanctuary* (National Theatre); *Canary* (Liverpool Playhouse/Hampstead); *Beautiful Thing* (Bush Theatre/Donmar/Duke of York's); *The Storm* (Almeida Theatre); *Top Girls* (Citizens Theatre); *M.A.D.* (Bush Theatre); *A Jamaican Airman Foresees His Death*, *Talking in Tongues*, *The Thickness of Skin*, *On Insomnia and Midnight* (Royal Court Theatre); *Leave Taking* (Women's Playhouse

Trust); *Hey Persephone!* (Aldeburgh Festival/Almeida Theatre).

Television directing credits include: *Steal*; *Normal People*; *Howards End*; *Fortitude*; *The Tunnel*; *Hit and Miss*; *White Girl*; *Doctor Who (Blink)*; *Wallander*; *Banglatown Banquet*; *Agatha Christie's Poirot*; *In A Land Of Plenty*.

Film directing credits include: *Beautiful Thing*.

OT **ORANGE TREE THEATRE**

A powerhouse of independent theatre

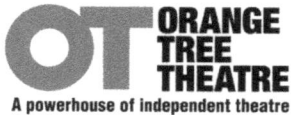

We are a local theatre with a global reputation.

A show at the Orange Tree is close-up magic: live, entertaining, unmissable. We're an intimate theatre with the audience wrapped around the stage. We believe in celebrating what it means to be human. We believe in putting people at the centre of the stories we tell. And we believe in the power of a writer's words, an actor's voice, and an audience's imagination to transport us to other worlds and other lives.

We punch above our weight to create world-class productions of new and contemporary drama, revitalise classics and re-discoveries, and introduce children and young people to the magic of theatre.

We are deeply rooted in our local community in South West London. We work with thousands of people aged 0 to 100 in Richmond and beyond through participatory theatre, bringing generations together to build confidence, connection, and joy. Our ground-breaking Primary Shakespeare and Shakespeare Up Close projects pack the theatre with children and ignite a spark to last a lifetime.

We're a registered charity (266128). With only 180 seats and no support from Arts Council England, we rely on the generosity of our audiences and donors to raise £650,000 a year. These funds support our outstanding work on stage and in the community and invest in the next generation of talent.

Artistic Director **Tom Littler**
Executive Director **Julie Weston**

orangetreetheatre.co.uk

LONDON BOROUGH OF
RICHMOND UPON THAMES

THEATRE OF THE YEAR   THE STAGE AWARDS

Hedda

Characters (*in order of appearance*)

Shona, **Hedda Gabler**'s *maid. Indian. Middle aged.*

Miss Julia Tesman, **George Tesman**'s *aunt. English. Middle aged.*

George Tesman, *English man. Film director.* **Hedda**'s *husband.*

Hedda Gabler, *dual heritage woman. Retired film star.*

Alice Smith, *English woman.*

John Brack, *English man. Film producer.*

Leonard Webb, *Dual heritage man. Writer/director.*

This version of **Hedda Gabler** *is set in a fashionable mews house in Chelsea, London in 1948, in the aftermath of the Second World War and Indian independence.*

Act I

DAY 1. September morning – around 9am.

A spacious drawing room in a house in Chelsea where all the action of the play will take place.

Shona *enters carrying a bouquet of flowers which she places on a surface. She stands in the middle of the room and pins up her hair, taking in her new surroundings with an anxious air. A doorbell rings.* **Shona** *exits to answer it.*

Julia *(O/S)*   Good morning! Shona – isn't it?

Shona *(O/S)*   Yes, Ma'am

Shona *enters, leading in* **Julia Tesman** *with her hat on.*

Shona   Memsahib is still sleeping.

Julia   Ah – the honeymooning couple.

Shona   The plane landed very late last night. And then when she got home, Memsahib had a lot to unpack before going to bed.

Julia   Let them rest. (*Looking around the room.*) It's so dark in here. Let's open some windows!

Julia *goes to the windows.*

Shona *(anxious)*   Ram! Ram!*

Memsahib is very particular about not having too much light . . .

Julia *pulls back some curtains.* **Shona** *stands back and watches disapprovingly.*

Julia   How long have you served as Hedda's maid – Shona?

Shona   Since the Memsahib was a child. I was her ayah.

---

* *Ram is one of the principle Hindu gods.*

Julia   You must have been very young yourself?

Shona   I am much older than I look, Ma'am.

Julia *looks closely at* **Shona**.

Julia   How much older?

Shona   If I told you, I might lose my job.

Julia   Lucky you. No grey hair and no wrinkles. What is your secret?

Shona   There is no hand to catch time.

Julia   I think black skin is more . . . elastic.

Beat as **Shona** *looks stone faced at the comment.*

Julia   My siblings and I were born in India, you know, Lahore, which apparently is in West Pakistan now! Spent a very happy childhood there. Came home ten years ago but I still miss India. Do you miss it?

Shona   There is a constant lack of sunshine here.

Julia   Which part of India are you from?

Shona   Calcutta.

Julia   Ah! I did visit there once when I was child. Big avenues, huge buildings. Victoria Memorial! Tell me, Shona, is your mistress very grand? I'm quite nervous of meeting her – only ever seen her on the silver screen.

Shona   She knows what she wants.

Julia   And what were her other husbands like? There were two before George, weren't there?

Shona   Three.

Julia (*surprised*)   Three?

Shona   The first one was very old, the second one was very young and the third one . . . he was a good man, but he had a terrible gambling habit, and he was unclean.

Julia (*alarmed*)   Unclean?

Shona   He could never tell the truth.

'Untruth is impure in any circumstances for it makes our inner nature unclean. This is a moral law, and it belongs to a higher plane.'

Julia   Oh! A religious quotation. How wonderful.

Shona   No. From India's national poet. Tagore.

Julia *looks utterly confused.*

Julia   My nephew had better keep his wits about him – married to General Gabler's daughter . . . I heard rumours he was quite terrifying.

Shona   He never frightened me – but he liked to terrorise people.

Julia   Didn't he die rather horribly?

Shona   In a hunting accident in the Sundarbans – chasing a Royal Bengal tiger but the tiger got the better of him.

Julia   And I read in a magazine that Hedda's mother died when she was very young?

Shona   Yes, Ma'am. She died in childbirth.

Julia   How tragic.

George Tesman *enters, humming to himself.*

Julia   Good morning, George.

George   Aunt Julia! Dear Auntie! Come so early!

Julia   I know – but I was excited to see you. Welcome home, George!

George *ignores* **Shona** *and greets* **Julia** *warmly.*

George   How lovely to see you. Strange being back here – so cold and dull.

Julia   Honestly, you wouldn't know that we were the heroic victors in war. Peace time is drab, impoverished and anything but glorious. And still so many shortages of everything.

Julia *takes off her hat and puts it down.*

George   What a gorgeous hat. Looks brand new!

Julia   I bought it so that Hedda wouldn't be ashamed of me if we went out together.

George   You're always so thoughtful, Auntie. How's Aunt Rina? Any improvement?

Julia   Poor thing. Still bedridden. So afraid of losing her – what will I do with my life, George, especially now that I don't have you to look after anymore?

Shona   I will see if the Memsahib needs help dressing.

Shona *exits.*

Julia   Never seen a maid like that! Seems so . . . high and mighty . . . unnerves me.

George   I try not to look at her, Auntie. Impossible to tell what she's thinking. Seems to stare right through me.

Julia   You should get an English maid for your wife.

George   I wish I could. It would be so much more appropriate but Hedda's very attached to the old coon.

Julia   George! You had an ayah when you were little. You loved her.

George   Ayah Nimbu was different.

Julia   Can't believe you're a married man, and you've hooked a beautiful film star! Hedda Gabler no less – Incredible!

George   Yes, I have several good friends about town who would like to stand in my shoes.

Julia   And such a long honeymoon!

It must have been a great financial undertaking?

George   I made some money from 'The Lighthouse'.

Julia   And you flew all the way back! The maid too?

George   The airline stopped her from travelling in the same class – blacks are not allowed. Thank goodness.

Julia   I did wonder – still – so expensive!

George   Yes, of course, it makes it a little more expensive – especially as Hedda has no money.

Julia   But I thought . . .?

George   She had to extricate herself from the film studio – had a five-film deal – only made two – had to pay them back. Those studios are cut throat. Cleaned her out. Sold her London flat and her house in California.

Julia   Oh dear.

George   But Hedda had to have this trip, Auntie! She really had to. Nothing else would have done.

Julia   More than five – nearly six months. George, don't you have something special to tell me? Some good news?

George (*excited*)   Yes, I'm shooting a big film and John Brack – the famous producer – has set up the finance.

Julia   I know him well.

George   He's an old friend of Hedda's. They've worked together before in the States. He's my friend now too – anyway, we're more or less good to go. Luckily for us, Brack was able to get favourable terms for me on this house. Wait – how on earth do you know John Brack?

Julia   He contacted me. I've given security for the furniture and all the rugs.

George   But what kind of security could you offer?

Julia   The trust fund – father left us.

George   Have you gone out of your mind? That trust fund is the only thing you and Aunt Rina have to live on.

Julia   Don't get all worked up about it. Mr Brack was the one who helped me arrange the whole thing. Just a formality, he said. A little mortgage.

George   That's all very well but . . .

Julia   You're doing so well in your career – think of it as a helping hand to begin with. We're only too happy.

George   Oh, Auntie – you're always sacrificing yourself for me.

George *kisses* **Julia**'s *hands.*

Julia   It's the only joy I have in this world – to help you along the road, my darling boy. There were some terrible, dark days – you were orphaned so young! But you've come through, nothing and no one to fear.

George   Thank you, Auntie.

Julia   Why did Hedda give up acting?

George   She said that she'd had enough of being a 'puppet actress'. Wanted to be her own woman.

Julia   Hedda Gabler – Hollywood legend – retired and married to my nephew! You see? Dreams can come true.

George   I have to keep pinching myself.

Julia   How did you manage to persuade her to marry you? To me, of course, you are my golden boy . . . but she has had three husbands!

George   No, two.

Julia   The maid told me it was three.

George   She must be mistaken.

Julia   Surely, she would know?

George   No. I am most definitely the third husband.

Julia   Oh, George! I hope she doesn't break your heart!

George   Don't worry about me, Auntie. I'm a big boy now.

Hedda *enters. She looks the epitome of refinement and distinction. She is dressed as a film star 'at home' – with all the grace of a glamorous hostess but she seems unused to her new surroundings and a little out of sorts.*

Julia (*approaching* **Hedda**)   Good morning, my dear Hedda! I am George's Aunt Julia.

Hedda   Miss Tesman. I have heard so much about you.

Julia   You must call me Auntie.

Hedda (*holds out her hand*)   That is kind of you, Miss Tesman, and so thoughtful of you to call on us so early!

Julia   Has the bride slept well in her new home?

Hedda   Tolerably.

George   Tolerably? That's a good one, Hedda! You were sleeping like a log when I got up.

Hedda   Of course one has always to accustom oneself to new surroundings, bit by bit. *Urgh* – that stupid maid's opened the curtains and let in a whole flood of sunshine. (*Calls out.*) Shona! Shona! If I've told you once, I've told you a thousand times about keeping the curtains drawn.

Julia   I will close them.

Hedda   No, George will do it. It will give a softer light.

George *draws the curtains.*

George   All right – all right.

Hedda   Do sit down, Miss Tesman?

Julia   No, thank you. Now that I have seen that everything is all right here – I must be getting home. My sister will be waiting for me, poor thing.

George   Give her my very best love, Auntie, and say I shall look in and see her later in the day.

Julia   I'll be sure to tell her.

Julia *stands back and looks at* **Hedda**, *almost drinking her in, which unnerves* **Hedda**.

Julia   You know something, Hedda, you really have the most beautiful eyes!

They remind me of my maid – Usha. Same beautiful deep brown eyes.

Hedda (*reacts sharply*)   Who put that nasty looking old hat there?

George   Hedda!

Hedda   Imagine, if any guests saw that! They'd think I had no taste!

George   Hedda! That's Auntie's.

Hedda   Is it?!

Julia (*taking up the hat*)   It is. And it's not old.

Hedda   I didn't really look that closely at it, Miss Tesman.

Julia (*putting on the hat*)   It's the first time I have worn it, the very first time.

George   And it's a beautiful hat – quite a stunner!

Hedda   Very handsome indeed.

George   Yes, isn't it? But Auntie, take a good look at Hedda before you go!

See how gorgeous she is! And have you noticed how healthy she is looking? Skin is luminous, and she's filled out a little.

Hedda   Filled out! Do you mind? I am exactly the same size as I was when we married.

George   So you insist, but I'm quite certain you are not. Don't you agree with me, Auntie?

Julia   Hedda is lovely, lovely – lovely.

Julia *goes up to* **Hedda**, *takes her head between both hands, draws it downwards, and kisses her hair.*

Julia   God bless and preserve, Hedda.

Hedda (*gently freeing herself*)   Let me go.

Julia   I shall come and see you every day.

Hedda *does not look pleased at the prospect but smiles nevertheless.*

Julia   Goodbye – goodbye!

Julia *exits and* **George** *accompanies her.*

George (*O/S*)   Do give my love to Aunt Rina. Thank you for dropping in.

Hedda *walks about the room, raising her arms and clenching her hands as if in desperation   Then she flings back the curtains and stands there looking out.*

George *enters and watches her for a while.*

Hedda   Look at the leaves on the trees, so yellow – so withered.

George   We are well into September now.

Hedda   September already.

George   Auntie wasn't her usual self.

Hedda   Isn't she always like that?

George   Maybe she was a little star struck meeting you?

Hedda   Do you think she was annoyed about the hat?

George.   Perhaps a little, not really.

Hedda   But what an idea, to pitch her hat about in the drawing room!

George   I can guarantee that Auntie won't do it again.

Hedda   I'll make it up to her. When you call this afternoon, you should invite her to dinner tonight.

George   I will. And there's one thing more you could do that would make her happy.

Hedda   What is it?

George   Couldn't you bring yourself to give her a little kiss when you meet? If only for my sake, Hedda? And call her Auntie.

Hedda   No, we have already discussed this. I shall try to call her Aunt Julia . . . if I remember – just be satisfied with that.

George   Now that you're part of the family – it would make her so happy.

Hedda (*gentle*)   Please don't be a nag. I'd like to get a new grand piano, George – put it in the front room. And we should have a butler if we are to entertain.

George (*a little concerned*)   Of course. Anything for you, Hedda.

Hedda (*takes up the bouquet*)   These flowers weren't here last night when we arrived.

George   Auntie must have brought them for you.

Hedda (*examining the bouquet*)   A visiting card. 'Shall return later in the day.'

George   Who is it from?

Hedda   It says Mrs Carl Humphries.

George   Carl Humphries' wife? I thought she died years ago?

Hedda   He married that little actress. At least, she called herself an actress.

George   Oh my goodness, yes! Alice . . . Alice Smith.

Hedda   Exactly. The girl with the irritating hair – constantly showing it off, swishing it around like a horse. Your old girlfriend – so I've been told.

George   That was well before I met you, Hedda, and it didn't last long.

Hedda   Strange that she should call on us. Hardly seen her since we we were on set . . . nine . . . ten years ago? Always forgetting her lines. Completely froze in front of the camera. I had a couple of scenes with her. So tedious.

George   Crippling stage fright, I recall. I haven't seen her for God knows how long. Humphries is a recluse, lives in a farmhouse in the middle of a field. I wonder how she can endure to live in such a God forsaken place.

Shona *enters.*

Shona   Memsahib, the lady who brought the flowers a little while ago, is here – again.

Hedda   Show her in.

Alice *enters.* **Hedda** *notices* **Alice**'s *nervous, anxious energy.*

Hedda   Alice! How lovely to see you again.

Alice   Yes, it's a very long time since we met, Mrs Tesman. And of course, you, George, I mean Mr Tesman.

Hedda *enjoys* **George**'s *embarrassment.*

George   Delighted to see you again . . . and Alice, do call me George.

Hedda   Thank you for the lovely flowers.

Alice   I would have come straight here yesterday afternoon – but I heard that you were abroad.

George   On our honeymoon.

Alice   Yes, of course. Congratulations . . . I arrived yesterday, about midday. I was quite in despair when I heard that you weren't at home.

Hedda   In despair! Why? I hope you're not in any trouble?

Alice   Yes, I am. And I don't know another living person that I can turn to.

Hedda   Something happened?

Beat.

Alice   Leonard Webb is in town.

Hedda *is intrigued and tries to hide her fascination with* **Alice***'s mention of* **Leonard***.*

Alice   He's been here a week already – in this dangerous city, all alone!

George   Probably up to no good.

Hedda   Alice, he's a grown man – what does this have to do with you?

Alice *has a startled air and speaks rapidly.* **Hedda** *can see something is not quite right.*

Alice   He was the children's tutor. That is my husband's. I don't have any.

Hedda   Your step-children?

Alice   Yes.

George   He's been . . . reliable . . . regular in his habits?

Alice   For the last year he has been completely sober.

George (*laughs*)   Leonard – sober?

Hedda (*laughs*)   Really?

Alice   Beyond reproach. He was a pilot with the R.A.F. during the war – a flying ace! Shot down over twenty enemy planes.

Hedda   Yes, I read about him. Could hardly believe it was Leonard they were describing. But what was a national hero doing tutoring children?

Alice   He had a mental breakdown after the war.

George   Poor Lenny. He must have witnessed some terrible things.

Alice   My husband knew him from before and gave him a job – to try and help him out.

Hedda   Lenny was always a very clever man.

George   Could have turned his hand to anything.

Alice   But now Leonard's here in the big city and we're very worried for him.

George   Why didn't he stay where he was?

Alice   After he finished his script, he got restless, almost frantic.

George   He's been writing again?

Alice   A wonderful script. He wrote it all whilst he was with us, within the last year.

George (*amazed*)   A new film?

Hedda (*jokes*)   Is there a good part in it – for me?

George   Always the actress, my darling. You've read it, Alice?

Alice   It is an extraordinary piece of work. Set in India. Very moving.

George   Unlikely to ever be made . . . I mean the film industry is on its knees at the moment. Very few things getting through – especially one about the colonies.

Hedda   Not the colonies anymore, George.

Alice   He wants to direct it and he's already got a lot of interest.

George   Isn't that good news, Hedda?

Hedda *seems unconvinced.*

Alice   If only he doesn't spoil his chances.

Hedda   Have you seen him here in town?

Alice   No, not yet. It was so difficult trying to find his address. But I finally managed to get hold of it this morning and I called on him but there was no response.

Hedda (*looks searchingly at* **Alice**)   A little odd, isn't it? Your husband sending you off into the city to track down his friend? Why didn't he come himself?

Alice   Carl has no time. And besides, I . . . I had some shopping to do.

Hedda   Of course, makes perfect sense.

Alice   George, you and Leonard used to be such good friends.

George   A long time ago.

Alice   You started out directing at the same time, he talks about you very fondly and has the greatest respect for you. So, if he comes here, which I'm sure he will, please keep an eye on him for me.

George   Of course.

Alice   Carl thinks the world of Leonard!

Hedda   You ought to write to Leonard now, George. Invite him over. He might not come of his own accord.

George   Good idea, Hedda.

Hedda   And the sooner the better. Now is as good a time as any.

Alice   Yes please! Thank you, thank you, George.

Alice *takes* **George**'*s hands and presses them.* **George** *is a little embarrassed whilst* **Hedda** *watches* **Alice** *with wry interest.*

George   No problem – I'll do it straight away. Do you have his address?

Alice *hurriedly takes a slip of paper from her pocket, and hands it to* **George**.

Alice   Here . . .

Hedda   Be sure you write him a good, long friendly letter.

George   Yes, I will.

Alice   But please, don't let him know that I asked you to invite him!

George   That goes without saying.

George *exits.*

Hedda   There! Two birds with one stone.

Alice *looks confused.*

Hedda   Now he's out of earshot, we can have a quiet chat.

Alice   There's nothing more to say – and I must be off now.

Hedda   Alice, there's a great deal more to say – it's perfectly obvious.

Alice *is desperate to get away.*

Alice   But, Mrs Tesman . . .

Hedda   The shopping can wait. It's early. Let's have a little 'girl' talk shall we? Now, why don't you tell me all about your home life.

Alice (*flustered*)   That's the last thing I want to talk about.

Hedda *turns up the volume on the charm.*

Hedda   You can talk to me. We're old friends – colleagues. Don't you remember that dreadful film we did together at Pinewood?

Alice   Yes, I had a tiny part. I was so frightened of you!

Hedda   Of me?

Alice   Before we went on set, when we met on the stairs, you always used to pull my hair.

Hedda   Did I?

Alice   You did. And once you said you were going to burn it all off.

Hedda   I was joking! You still have a beautiful head of hair.

Alice   It scared the living daylights out of me. That's why I couldn't remember my lines. I was such a fool in those days. You, on the other hand, always had star quality. Anyone could see that.

Hedda   I was lucky. I never had to play crowd parts. Just hanging around a studio on chance must in the end prove dreadfully dispiriting, I should imagine.

Alice   You're such an amazing actress.

Hedda   Thank you.

Alice   Comes naturally to you, like breathing air.

Hedda   I'm retired now.

Alice   Really? You're still so beautiful . . . why would you give it all up?

Hedda   I'm taking a little rest from it all.

Alice   So you're not retired?

Hedda *changes the subject.*

Hedda We used to be such good friends, and we called each other by our Christian names.

Alice I don't think we did.

Hedda We did, and now we're going to renew our old friendship.

Hedda *kisses* **Alice** *on the cheek.*

Hedda There now! You must call me Hedda.

Alice You are so good. I am not used to kindness.

Hedda And I will call you my darling Alison.

Alice Alice.

Hedda Alice, yes, that's what I said. So, let me get this right – you're not used to kindness, Alice? Not even in your own home?

Alice I've never really had a home.

Hedda That's what I thought.

Alice (*helplessly*)   Nothing – no home ever.

Hedda How did you end up marrying Carl Humphries?

Alice It was after 'Courageous'.

Hedda 'Courageous'?

Alice The film we made?

Hedda Oh! Silly me.

Alice I was so awful in it, and I finally came to the realisation that my temperament wasn't suited to acting. I decided to go back to teaching and I went to the Humphries' as a governess just after war broke out. His wife – his late wife – was very ill and rarely left her room. So, I ended up looking after the house as well.

Hedda And eventually you became the mistress of the house.

Alice   Yes, soon after the first Mrs Humphries died, I married Carl. (*Sadly.*) That was five years ago.

Alice *looks away upset.* **Hedda** *watches her like a hawk.*

Hedda   And how long has Leonard been in the neighbourhood?

Alice   A year.

Hedda *sees a glimmer of guilt and she starts to home in on* **Alice**.

Hedda   Did you know him from before?

Alice   Only by name. I saw his early films.

Hedda   But you got to know him?

Alice   Yes, he came to us every day. He gave the children lessons. I couldn't manage it all myself.

Hedda   It must have been hard. And your husband?

Alice   Always working, writing his plays, hates being disturbed by anyone.

Hedda   Does your husband treat you well?

Alice   I am sure he thinks he does.

Hedda   I met Carl once. He came on set to visit my husband. Not George, my first husband – Howard.

Alice   The famous director?

Hedda   Yes. Carl struck me as quite old. At least as old as Howard.

Alice   Twenty-five years older than me and we have absolutely nothing in common.

Hedda *is slightly taken aback by* **Alice***'s passion.*

Hedda   But he's fond of you all the same?

Alice   I really don't know. I'm useful – cheap labour. He repels me.

Hedda   That's a terrible thing to say.

Alice   That's how he makes me feel. Doesn't really care for any one but himself . . . maybe a little for the children.

Hedda   And he cares for Leonard?

Alice   Leonard? Why are you asking about . . . (him)?

Hedda   You said Carl was very fond of Leonard – which is why he sent you all the way here to look for him.

Beat as **Alice** *is on the brink of confessing.* **Hedda** *waits hungrily.*

Alice   I didn't tell Carl that I was leaving.

Hedda *is at once impressed and shocked.*

Hedda   Ahh!

Alice   Hedda! The future looks so bleak and lonely. When he touches me, my body freezes. I can't stand it.

Hedda   That is bad. And then?

Alice   I packed a few belongings quietly – the essentials, and then I left.

Hedda   Just like that?

Alice   Yes, and I took the train to town.

Hedda   Little shy Alice! I can hardly believe that you had the nerve to do such a brave thing!

Alice   What else could I do?

Hedda   But what do you think your husband will say when you go back again?

Alice (*steely*)   I will never go back to him again.

Hedda   And the children? Won't you miss them?

Alice (*shrugs wearily*)   Five years, Hedda – I did my duty as a wife, housekeeper and a governess. Never a mother. I'm done with that now

Hedda   Then you've really . . . in all seriousness . . . you've run away for good?

Alice   I didn't have a choice.

Hedda (*fascinated*)   But to take flight so openly. Aren't you worried about what people will think of you? The gossip? The scandal!

Alice   They can say what they like.

Hedda (*amazed*)   You really don't care, do you?

Alice   It's my life.

Beat.

Hedda   And what are your plans now? How will you earn a living?

Alice   I don't know yet. I only know that I must live wherever Lenny is – if I am to live at all.

Hedda   'If I am to live at all'? My dear Alice, so dramatic! I think you *are* an actress after all.

How did this – this 'friendship' between you and 'Lenny' come about?

Alice   It happened, day by day, bit by bit. We became closer. He told me that after the war he'd been unbalanced and that he got muddled.

Hedda   And he was a very heavy drinker.

Alice   He was. The war did something to him – made him melancholy and he drank to drown his nightmares. After a few months with us, he slowly gave up his old behaviour – not because I asked him to, I'd never dare to do that. But he saw how much I hated his self-destructive ways – the whoring, the partying and fighting and so he dropped them. I slowly gained some kind of control over him.

Hedda (*entranced*)   Control?

Alice   He needed someone strong who could understand him.

Hedda *conceals an involuntary smile of scorn.*

Hedda   Then Alice, you have 'reclaimed' him.

Alice   He says the same. In the meantime, he has given me so much confidence, to think, to imagine, to use my intelligence.

Hedda   Did he give you lessons too, then?

Alice   Not exactly. But he talked to me as an equal about politics, history, war, humanity, religion. He is so bright, Hedda! When his mind is clear, the ideas, the thoughts, the knowledge that come forth from his lips is astounding. He's so passionate – it's hard to resist. Then came the happy day when I started to share his work.

Hedda   How extraordinary.

Alice   Yes! When he was writing anything, we worked on it together.

Hedda (*knowing*)   Like two good comrades.

Alice   Comrades! Hedda, that is the very word he used! I ought to feel completely happy, but I can't because I don't know if it will last.

Hedda   Don't you trust him?

Alice   There's the shadow of the war which hangs over him and there's a woman that stands between us.

Hedda   Who?

Alice   Someone he knew in his past. Someone he's never really been able to forget. He has only once mentioned her – vaguely . . .

Hedda   And what did he say?

Alice   He said that when they parted, she threatened to shoot him with a pistol.

Hedda   How absurd.

Hush! Here comes George.

George *enters with a letter in his hand.* **Hedda** *settles herself but is quite churned up.*

George   The letter's done.

Hedda   Good. I think Alice wants to go now. I'll walk her out.

George   I say, Hedda, do you think Shona could post the letter?

Hedda (*takes the letter*)   I will tell her to.

Shona *enters.*

Shona   Mr Brack is here and would like to see Memsahib and Sir.

Hedda   Yes, show him in. And Shona, put this letter in the post.

Shona (*taking the letter*)   Yes, Memsahib.

Hedda (*sharply to* **Shona**)   Quick as you can.

Shona *shows* **Brack** *into the room, glances at the name on the envelope and then exits.*

Brack   May one call so early in the day?

Hedda   Of course one may. You're our third visitor this morning!

George   You are welcome at any time. (*Introducing him.*) Mr Brack – Mrs Humphries, Carl's wife.

Brack *surreptitiously looks* **Alice** *up and down. She looks uneasy.*

Brack   Delighted. I know your husband well.

Alice   Yes – I believe you worked on a film together a while ago.

Hedda   It's nice to see you in daylight, John!

Brack   Do I look even more handsome than usual?

Hedda   Devastatingly.

Brack *laughs.*

George   What do you think of Hedda? Doesn't she look positively glowing?

Brack   Hedda always glows – a little flushed, I might say? (*To* **Hedda**.) Something's got your blood racing this morning?

Hedda   Just very pleased to see you . . . all. We must thank you, John, for helping to acquire this lovely house for us.

Brack   No trouble at all.

Hedda   If George had his way, we'd be living in the sticks, just so we could be near the studios.

Brack   You need to be in London, at the heart of society, close to where I can keep an eye on you.

Hedda   Exactly.

Alice is impatient to be off. I shall be back again presently.

Mutual goodbyes. **Alice** *and* **Hedda** *exit.*

Brack   Is your starry wife satisfied?

Tesman   Yes, we can't thank you sufficiently. Of course, she talks of a little re-arrangement here and there, and one or two things are still wanting. She wants a butler and a grand piano!

Brack   She doesn't even play the piano. This place is quite pricey. Chelsea no less. I did advise you to get something less extravagant.

George   But that would never have done for Hedda. You know what she's like – I couldn't possibly ask her to put up with a shabby suburban house.

Brack   And there lies the problem.

George   We'd both seen this house one night as we were walking and set our hearts on it. Besides, it can't be long before we get going. I'm desperate to get back behind a camera. Any day soon now?

Brack   Nothing definite, but . . . I do have one piece of news for you.

Your old friend, Leonard Webb, has arrived in London.

George   I heard. Apparently, he's sobered up and written a new film script.

Brack   Yes.

George   And according to Alice it's good.

Brack   The word out there is it's rather brilliant, actually.

George   You've read it?

Brack   Not yet. But Carl has – and he wrote to me, described the narrative and central character's journey, insisted that I should read it. He thinks Leonard's written an extraordinary script.

George   Carl Humphries? But he's a playwright – what would he know?

Brack   Carl is very widely read and advises me regularly. And my business partner is a big fan of Leonard's early films – he's very excited to read it.

George   I thought Lenny had disappeared for good.

Brack   That's what everyone thought.

George   Do you think anyone will want to do his film? I hear it's set in India. There's no appetite for such a thing – is there?

Brack   You'd be surprised. It's very current. The world has changed, George – recent independence – a new country – a fresh perspective.

George   Very expensive, I should imagine. Lenny burnt all his bridges years ago in film making – I wonder how he'll make a living?

Hedda *enters – her mood subdued and thoughtful.*

Hedda (*with a touch of scorn*)   George is always worrying about how people are to make their living.

George   Hedda dear, we were talking about poor Leonard.

Hedda *sits in the chair beside the stove.*

Hedda (*indifferent*)   Were you? What's wrong with him?

Brack   Nothing, but he's got a new script in the works. And, let's not forget – the man had immense talent once.

George   At one time, yes! But he put an end to all of that with his drinking, shouting at actors, making actresses cry on set, not turning up to shoots – behaving like a drunken beast.

Brack   No self-discipline. He lost me a lot of cash.

Hedda   But there may be a glimmer of hope for him. According to Alice, they have reclaimed him up at the Humphries'.

George   It'll be interesting to see how he's turned out. I have just invited him over to ours this evening.

Brack   George! What about the party tonight at my place – you gave me your word, and it's in your honour!

Hedda   Had you forgotten, George?

George   Oh no! Apologies, John. Perhaps Lenny could join us.

Beat as **Brack** *collects his thoughts.*

Brack   I have something rather delicate to share with you both. As I said, my business partner's very interested in Leonard's script. If it's as good as people think it is – he wants to back it.

Hedda   And what about George's film?

Brack   There's still a chance for George's film down the line, but my partner's requested we set it aside for the moment.

Hedda *turns away, silent and disengaged – bored with the inevitability of it all.*

George   Hang on – 'set it aside'?

Brack   We have a slot at the end of this year to finance and produce a film.

George   Which you said would be my film.

Brack   Yeah, but there may be some fierce competition – from Leonard.

Hedda (*very still*)   It'll be like a duel.

George (*to* **Hedda**)   How can you be so calm about it?

Hedda   I'm not – I'm very eager to see who wins.

George (*aghast*)   You would dump my script on the promise of another one you haven't even read?

Brack   It's not finalised, but I'm obliged to pursue all avenues.

George   We married on the strength of these prospects, Hedda and I, and run deep into debt – apparently borrowed money from Auntie too, John – though I knew nothing about the arrangement. Good heavens!

Brack   Nothing is confirmed until we read Leonard's script – but I wanted to let you know. Hedda, this may change your plans as to the little purchases you were going to make.

Hedda   It makes no difference and it's actually none of your business.

Brack   Indeed. Then there's nothing more to be said.

Hedda *lays back in the chair, almost bored. She holds out her hand to* **Brack**.

Hedda   Goodbye, Mr Brack.

Brack *takes her hand.*

Brack   I'll come and pick you up, George, later for the party.

George   Oh yes, yes –

Brack *exits.* **George** *is upset.*

George   This news has quite upset me. We shouldn't have rushed into marriage and set up house based on mere expectations. We were going to go into society – to keep open house. I was so looking forward to it, Hedda! But for the present we shall have to get on without society, only invite Auntie now and then. I wanted you to lead such an utterly different life.

Hedda   So, no butler?

George   That would be out of the question.

Hedda   And the grand piano I was to have in the front room?

George   I'm afraid not.

Hedda *sinks to the floor and lies on her back, silent.* **George** *watches her afraid.*

George   It's not the end of the world. Brack did say it wasn't definite. It's just a hiccup. Hedda, say something.

Hedda   Well, I shall have one thing at least to kill time with.

George   A little hobby. Yes. What is it, Hedda?

Hedda   My pistols, George. General Gabler's pistols.

Act II

SAME DAY – 5pm.

The **Tesmans'** *drawing room, as in Act I. Evening is drawing in and the light is beginning to fade. A pistols' case lies empty.* **Hedda** *holds one pistol. Opposite her,* **Shona** *loads the other with practiced ease.*

Shona Not sure why you want these. You'll bring the local constabulary here if you shoot them off.

Hedda Just a bit of harmless target practice.

Hedda *and* **Shona** *swap pistols and* **Shona** *gets busy loading the second pistol.*

Shona Why do you hang on to them?

Hedda *points the pistol at something.*

Hedda To remind me of Daddy, so I never forget where I came from.

Shona How will you feel when you see that man again?

Hedda I'm rather curious to be honest. He was an absolute wreck the last time I saw him.

Shona A dreadful drunk.

Hedda Yes. Anyway. I'm a married woman now. It doesn't matter how I feel.

Shona It was your choice to marry – again.

Hedda I had to! George will provide me with stability. To go through life without a companion by my side is inconceivable.

Shona And I'm not enough?

Hedda (*jokes*) You're my mother, not a man.

Shona And men never fail to bring you such delight.

Hedda   At least George talks to me – once we were married, the others never did.

Shona   Happy is the woman whose husband does not speak to her.

Hedda   George is perfectly pleasant and attentive to my needs.

Shona   You married beneath you. He's a terrible, pedestrian director.

And utterly charmless.

Hedda   Don't start.

Shona   All those dull propaganda films he made during the war. Euch. And he despises me.

Hedda   You don't exactly make an effort with him.

Shona   That is because every time he opens his mouth, he sounds like a first-class donkey – *Akabare gadha.* (*Bengali.*)

Hedda (*can't help but laugh*)   Stop it.

Shona   You'll have to make the best of it now.

Hedda *paces, then takes the other pistol from* **Shona**. *Her movements are restless, unresolved.* **Shona** *watches her.*

Shona   Why don't you just go back to work? You'll feel better.

Hedda   I don't want to pretend anymore.

Shona   You're an actress. Pretending is your job.

Hedda   I'm sick of hiding and lying.

Shona   Don't talk rubbish. You've had a charmed life, risen high up the ladder of success. Other women would kill to have your career.

Hedda   At what cost though?

I can't do that anymore.

Shona   Child – you're too spoilt. Always excitement with you. You have to learn to be still sometimes and remember your dream.

Hedda   Maybe – if I can do it my own way – on my terms . . .

Shona   What are you saying?

Hedda   If I could speak the truth, I could free myself.

Shona   The mouth that speaks truth earns many enemies.

Hedda *pulls the curtains open, then quickly closes them again, impatiently.*

Hedda   I want to be back in front of a camera – speaking extraordinary words and turning my face to the light. It's all I've ever wanted. What if I never act again – if I never get another part? Unimaginable! I can't bear not to be working. I need to work!

Shona   So what is the problem?

Why do you torture yourself? This fantasy of yours is self-destructive.

We have kept the secret going for years! You reveal your Indian side, and everyone will reject and ridicule you – including your lovely aunty and new husband. I overheard him calling me a 'coon' today.

Hedda *smarts.*

Shona   What do you think he'd call you?

Hedda *is quiet.*

Shona   Stop all this thinking. It will all work out – you'll see. And whatever happens, I will be here by your side. Have courage.

Shona *exits.* **Hedda** *walks about the room for a moment on her own – frustrated by her dilemma.*

Hedda (*anguished*)   Courage?

She hears a rustle outside from the garden. **Hedda** *gathers herself and stands by the open door, aiming.*

(*Calls out.*) Hullo again, Mr Brack!

Brack (*O/S, calls back*)   Hedda!

Hedda   Look out! I'm going to shoot you.

Brack (*O/S*)   No, no, no! What are you doing? Don't aim at me!

Hedda   This is what comes of sneaking in by the back way.

Hedda *fires.*

Brack (*O/S*)   ARE YOU COMPLETELY UNHINGED?

Hedda   Dear me, I didn't hit you – did I?

Brack (*closer*)   Put the pistols down immediately!

Hedda   Come in then.

Brack *enters. He is furious and visibly shaken. Dressed smartly in his dinner suit.*

Brack   What the hell do you think you're playing at? Mad woman!

Brack *gently takes the pistols out of* **Hedda***'s hand and calms down.*

Brack   What a way to welcome an old friend to the house! Allow me, madam! (*Looks around.*) Where is the case? Here it is.

(*Lays the pistols in and shuts the case.*) Enough of your dangerous games.

Hedda   Then what in heaven's name would you have me do with myself?

Brack   Where's George?

Hedda   The minute he finished lunch, he tore off to his aunts.

Brack   So we're alone?

Hedda   Just you, me . . . and the maid.

Brack   If I had known. I would have come a little – earlier.

Hedda   Then you would have found no one here; I have been in my room, changing.

Brack   And isn't there a little chink in the door through which we could have communicated?

Hedda   You forgot to arrange one.

Brack   That was stupid of me too.

Hedda   We will just have to sit here and wait. George will be a while.

Beat.

Well?

Brack   Well?

Hedda   I spoke first.

Brack   I've been longing to see to you again.

Hedda (*flirtatious*)   I have been wishing the same.

Brack   And I thought you were busy basking in the delights of your honeymoon!

Hedda   I was excruciatingly bored – apart from the occasional trip to the movies. I saw 'Oliver Twist' twice.

Brack   And George went with you?

Hedda   Yes. But you know what he's like – forensically analysing a film as if it's a scientific study. Leeches the joy out of it. But then George is a specialist film craftsman.

Brack   Undeniably.

Hedda   And specialists are not at all amusing to travel with. Not in the long run, at any rate.

Brack   Not even the specialist one happens to love?

Hedda   Such a sentimental word!

Brack   You could have had absolutely anyone.

Hedda   There is something solid about George, he is a thoroughly good creature . . . and I had positively danced myself tired, John.

Brack   Good and reliable.

Hedda   Unlike you.

Brack   What are you implying?

Hedda   I saw the way you ogled Alice.

Brack   Hedda – I'm flattered, you're jealous!

Hedda   Not in the slightest.

Brack   Is it respectability you're looking for?

Hedda   It was more than my other adorers were prepared to do for me, my dear John.

Brack (*laughing*)   I can't answer for all the rest, but as for myself, you know quite well that I have always entertained a deep respect for marriage as an institution, Mrs Tesman.

Hedda   I have never cherished any hopes with respect to you.

Brack   All I need is a pleasant and intimate circle of friends where I can be useful in one way or another and can come and go freely as a trusted friend . . .

Hedda   Of the husband, do you mean?

Brack   To be quite frank, of the wife, preferably. But of the husband too, in the second place. Such a triangular friendship – if I may call it so – is really a great convenience for all the parties.

Hedda   I often longed for a third person on that honeymoon.

Brack   Fortunately your honeymoon is over now.

Hedda   Oh no, I'm stuck in the train carriage, and I've only just arrived at the station.

Brack   Surely the passenger has to jump out and stretch her legs a little?

Hedda   I never jump out.

Brack   Come, come, everyone has to have some light relief.

Hedda   I would never do it. I'd rather stay put, in the carriage.

Brack   But suppose a third person were to jump in and join the couple?

A trusted, sympathetic friend.

Hedda   With a wealth of charm and amusing anecdotes. And of course, gossip.

Brack   And not the least bit of a specialist!

Hedda   Yes, that would be a relief indeed. Some entertainment.

Brack   I can do more than *talk* entertainingly.

Hedda   Promises, promises.

Brack *hears the front door.*

Brack   The triangle is complete.

George *enters, hesitating awkwardly for a moment when he sees* **Brack**.

George   Hullo – are you here already, John? Shona didn't tell me.

Brack   I came in through the garden.

George   I must change my clothes. (*To* **Brack**.) I say, we've got time, haven't we?

Brack.   There's no hurry.

George   I will take my time then. Hedda, Auntie isn't coming this evening.

Hedda   Is it the hat business that's keeping her away?

George   Oh, not at all. Aunt Rina is very ill.

Hedda   She's always ill.

George   Yes, but today she's much worse than usual, poor dear.

Hedda   Then it's only natural that her sister should remain with her. I must bear my disappointment.

George   Despite that, you can't imagine how Auntie was delighted to meet you – and she commented on how . . . healthy . . . you were looking.

Hedda *looks away, deeply annoyed.*

George *exits.*

Brack   What hat were you talking about?

Hedda   It was a little episode with Julia this morning. She'd thrown down her hat and I pretended I didn't know it was hers and said it was a hideous looking thing.

Brack   Hedda, how could you? To such a nice old lady, too!

Hedda   These impulses come over me all of a sudden, and I can't stop them.

Brack   You're unhappy – that's the trouble.

Hedda   I don't know of a single reason why I should be happy. Perhaps you can give me one?

Brack   Because you have your dream house?

Hedda That old story?

Brack Is there nothing in it, then?

Hedda Last summer, when I was here in London, George was very useful to me – he'd always gallantly see me home after parties.

Brack Unfortunately, I was going quite the opposite direction.

Hedda That's true. You were certainly going in another direction last summer.

What was her name again?

Brack Carry on with your story.

Hedda We happened to pass here one evening; George, poor creature was tying himself in knots trying to make conversation, so I took pity on the man.

Brack *You* took pity?

Hedda Yes, I did. To help him out of his torment, I happened to say, in pure thoughtlessness, that I should like to live here.

So, you see, it was this enthusiasm for the house that first constituted a bond of sympathy between George and me. From that came our engagement and our marriage, and our honeymoon, and all the rest of it.

Brack Priceless! But surely you must feel different now that he's made it so homely for you?

Hedda The rooms all smell of lavender and dried rose leaves.

But perhaps it's Auntie that has brought that scent with her.

There is an odour of mortality about it. The most intolerable thing is . . . everlastingly having to be with . . . with one and the same person. Day and night.

You cannot imagine how horribly I shall bore myself here.

Brack London is a very vibrant city. There are clubs and bars.

Hedda I used to work in them when I first arrived here. Can't stand the places. All those disgusting old men with their wandering hands. I was so young.

Brack Poor, poor Hedda.

Hedda There we have it. This dull, middle-class world I've got into. Makes my life so wretched! So absolutely ludicrous! Because that's what it is.

Brack Maybe you could find a new vocation in life?

Hedda I have a vocation. The silver screen!

Brack But you retired from it – in a very public way.

Hedda You know why I left. The studio had too much control over me.

Brack Was that it? You never did tell me the details.

Hedda You don't need to know everything.

Brack Don't you miss California?

Hedda I do . . . but . . .

Brack You were utterly comfortable there.

Hedda Never entirely comfortable. Everything about the place seemed exaggerated. The sun was too big and too hot. The flowers were too vivid, too colourful to be real. The buildings and homes too ornate to work and live in, the sea too blue to be natural. Everything had that look to it. Even the people. I never saw so many lovely girls in one place before. Or so many handsome men. To the stranger at the gates, there seems to be a sort of impermanent air about the whole place.

Brack Let's not pretend – you're dying to get back in the game.

Hedda   Only on my terms.

Brack   What are your terms?

Hedda *pauses as if to say something but then doesn't.* **Brack** *watches her hesitation with curiosity.*

Brack   I have a proposition for you. I can help you.

Hedda   And what would that cost me, John?

Brack   You can pay me back however you wish. If that's what you want.

Hedda   What is your proposition?

Brack   A part in Leonard's film. The starring role of course.

Hedda   You haven't even read the script.

Brack   As I said, I know the storyline and the journey of the main character – a woman. If Leonard's writing like he used to, this could be something extraordinary. My production company would jump at the chance – we're a free agent, no studio ties.

Hedda   What about George?

Brack   He'll get over it. You'll make good money, get your name out there again, buy that piano – maybe even have someone to answer the door.

Hedda   And I wouldn't be bored.

What is the part?

Brack   But surely, you're most likely to have another very serious claim on you? A new – shall we say – responsibility – little Mrs Hedda?

Hedda (*angrily*)   Never. I have no yearning for responsibilities like that.

Brack   Why shouldn't you, like most other women, have a natural aptitude for . .?

Hedda   Oh, be quiet! There is only one thing in the world I have any aptitude for.

Brack   And what is that, if I may ask?

Hedda   For boring myself to death.

Beat.

What is the role in Leonard's film?

George *enters dressed for the party.* **Hedda** *fusses with his tie.*

Hedda   Oh! Don't you look dashing!

George (*pleased as punch*)   Thank you! Hedda – any message from Lenny?

Hedda   No.

George   He'll be here soon.

Brack   You really think he will come?

George   Yes, I'm sure he will. So, if you don't mind, I should wait for him as long as possible.

Brack   We have plenty of time yet. None of my guests will arrive before seven or half-past.

George   In the meantime, we can keep Hedda company, until he comes.

Hedda   And if all else fails – Mr Webb can keep me company.

Brack   What do you mean, 'if all else fails'?

Hedda   If he doesn't want to go with you and George, he can stay here with me and Alice – she's coming over later. The three of us can drink tea together.

George   Oh yes, that will be good.

Brack   And perhaps the safest bet for him.

Hedda   Why so?

Brack   Remember, Hedda, how you used to say my parties could knock a man clean off the straight and narrow.

Hedda   But Lenny has self-control these days –

George   If he's truly reformed, he'll be fine.

Brack   Well then, we should invite him along.

Shona *enters.*

Shona   There's a gentleman asking if you are at home, Memsahib.

Hedda   Show him in, Shona.

Leonard *enters. He is surprised and thrown to see everyone and hesitates, slightly awkward.* **Shona** *gives him a dirty look and exits.* **George** *approaches* **Leonard** *and shakes him warmly by the hand.*

George   Lenny – at last, we meet again!

Leonard   Thanks for your most kind letter, George. (*Approaching* **Hedda**.) Will you shake hands with me too, Mrs Tesman?

Hedda (*taking his hand*)   How lovely to see you, Leonard.

Brack *steps forward too and shakes hands with* **Leonard**.

Leonard   John – good to see you again.

Brack   Not since the good old days.

George   Please, Lenny, don't stand on ceremony – you are most welcome here anytime – isn't he, Hedda? I hear London's back on the cards.

Leonard   I hope so.

George   Excellent.

Leonard Webb – a flying ace! Shot down over twenty enemy planes. We read all about you.

You're a war hero!

Leonard   I'm lucky to be alive. Many weren't.

George   And now, Lenny, you're writing again. That's just wonderful. Wonderful for the cinema audiences!

Leonard   Thank you, George. Good of you to say so.

George   I'm very much looking forward to reading your new script . . .

Leonard *takes a script out of his pocket.*

Leonard (*excited*)   This is the script I have put my life and soul into. George, I would particularly love you to read it.

George   I'd be honoured to. What is it about?

Leonard.   I don't want to spoil it for you.

George   It's all hand-written!

Leonard   I rewrote it in a frenzy last night – it needs to be typed up. I changed it but it still needs a better ending.

Brack   I would very much like to read it too, Leonard.

Leonard   Of course. I brought it with me, thinking I might read it this evening.

In the past, George, your notes were always incisive.

Hedda   What about me? Don't I get a read of this miraculous script too?

Leonard   I would be most honoured, Mrs Tesman.

George   Sorry, this evening's a bit tricky after all.

Leonard   Another time then. There's no hurry.

Brack   There is a little gathering at my place tonight – to toast George's marriage to the lovely Hedda.

Leonard   In that case, I won't keep you.

Brack   Please, do join us?

Leonard   I can't – thank you.

Brack   You must! We're a fairly select group – just a few old friends.

Brack   I assure you we shall have a lively time.

Leonard   I don't doubt it, but I really can't . . .

Brack   You could bring your script with you, and read it to us all at my place.

George   Yes, that's a great idea.

Hedda   Leonard doesn't want to attend your raucous party, he would much rather stay, have supper and perhaps read the script to me.

Leonard   With you, Mrs Tesman?

Hedda   And with Alice – Mrs Humphries. I invited her to dine with me.

Leonard   I bumped into Alice this morning.

Hedda   We can all have a lovely meal together. You remember what an excellent cook Shona is?

Leonard   Yes, indeed. My mouth is watering at the memory of her cooking.

George   You know the maid?

Hedda   Shona's been with me forever, George.

Brack   Hedda – out of curiosity – How *did* you and Leonard get acquainted?

Hedda (*thinking on her feet*)   My father, the General, was friends with Leonard's father.

Brack   In India?

Leonard   Yes, though I was sent off to boarding school in England quite young.

George   I did not know that. How extraordinary! So, you're childhood friends?

Leonard   I wouldn't presume to say 'friends'. Even back then, Hedda Gabler barely noticed my existence.

They all laugh. **Brack** *looks a little put out but covers it up.*

Hedda   Anyway Leonard, you can see Alice home at the end of the evening.

Leonard   That's true. Thank you very much, Mrs Tesman. In that case, I'll stay here.

George   Lenny, let me get this straight. You've written a script, which John and others are chomping at the bit to read, but you've now improved it?

Leonard (*sceptical*)   Are you interested in my scribblings, John?

Brack   I wouldn't be doing my job if I weren't.

Leonard   It isn't ready – still needs a lot of work. Which is why I would welcome your thoughts on it, George, so I can work on the next draft.

Brack   How long will it take to finish?

Leonard   A few months maybe.

Brack   Why will it take so long?

Leonard   I need time to perfect my writing.

George   You mean you're not going to compete with me?

Leonard (*confused*)   I'm sorry?

George   You know that John's only got one production slot this autumn, I had hoped it would be my film but now that you're back in the game . . .

Leonard (*sincere*)   I have no intention of competing with you, George.

George *looks at* **Brack** *who doesn't react.*

Leonard   I've waited so long, worked so hard, it's important to get the script absolutely perfect. I only want to make a film which is my best work so I will wait until I am satisfied.

George   Why, bless me! Hedda! Just fancy – Leonard is not going to stand in our way!

Hedda   Our way? Leave me out of it.

George   John – what do you say to this?

Brack   Leonard is a true artist with integrity. I'd still like to see the script for myself, though.

George   Yes, certainly But all the same . . . the storm has passed.

Hedda *quickly takes charge.*

Hedda   Gentlemen – a little aperitif? Will you take a glass of cold punch?

Brack   Delighted.

George   A capital idea, Hedda! Just the thing!

Hedda   Will you join them, Leonard?

Leonard   No, thank you. Nothing for me.

Brack   Cold punch isn't poison as far as I know.

Leonard   Perhaps not for everyone.

Hedda   I will entertain Leonard in the meantime.

George   Yes, yes, Hedda dear, you do that.

George *and* **Brack** *exit chatting as they go.*

Hedda *produces a small album and switches on a light.*

Hedda   Would you care to look at my scrap book? It has all my notices and photographs from my work over the years.

Leonard *approaches, stops and looks at her.*

Hedda (*pointing to a photograph*)   This was from my first film – look how innocent I look!

Leonard   Hema!

Hedda   Hush, Lenny . . .

Leonard (*repeats softly*)   Hema Gabler!

Hedda   That was my name in the old days.

Leonard   Then I must never say Hema Gabler again?

Hedda   No. You should practise saying Mrs Tesman.

Leonard   Hedda Gabler married to George Tesman!

Hedda   Yes, and so the world turns.

Leonard   Oh, darling Hema – how could you throw yourself away!

Hedda   I thought you were old friends with George? You traitor.

Leonard   He's not good enough for you.

Hedda   Neither are you. George is a hundred times more reliable.

George *enters the room and approaches them.*

Hedda (*hears him coming and says in an indifferent tone*)   And this is me with Charles Laughton.

George   Look how beautiful you are.

Leonard   Spellbinding.

George   Hedda, dear, would you like a little punch? For yourself at least?

Hedda   Yes please.

George   Of course.

George *exits again.*

Leonard   Darling Hema . . . how could you go and do this?

Hedda (*apparently absorbed in the scrap book*)   If you continue to call me darling or by that name, I won't talk to you.

Leonard   Can't I even say it even when we are alone?

Hedda   No. You can think it, but you mustn't say it.

Leonard   In case I offend your love for George?

Hedda   Love? What an idea!

Leonard   You don't love him then!

Hedda   But I won't be unfaithful to him.

Leonard   Hema . . .

Hedda   Hush!

George *enters with a tray with two glasses and a jug of punch. He pours out two glasses.*

George   Here you are!

Hedda   We do have a maid, George.

George   I like waiting on you, Hedda. It's fun.

Hedda   You have poured out two glasses. Leonard said he wouldn't have any.

George   No, but Alice will soon be here, won't she?

Hedda   Of course, Alice.

George   Had you forgotten about her?

Hedda   We were so absorbed in these photographs.

Hedda *shows* **George** *another picture.*

Hedda   Do you remember me in this one?

George *looks at the photograph.*

George   Titania in 'Midsummer Night's Dream'. How could I forget?

Leonard   How could anyone? You were magnificent in that.

George   She was.

George *exits again.*

Leonard   When we were friends, wasn't there a flicker of your love for me?

Hedda (*remembering*)   When I look back on it, I think of us as good comrades – two intimate friends who could tell each other – intimate things. At least you revealed all your darkest secrets to me.

Leonard   It was you who goaded me to reveal everything.

Hedda   It was a beautiful, secretive and brave friendship.

Leonard   It was, wasn't it? When I used to come to your father's house in Calcutta, in the afternoon to help you with elocution and the General sat over at the window reading his papers, with his back towards us and Shona fussed around us with tea and sweetmeats.

Hedda   Us two on the corner sofa . . .

Leonard   Always with the same magazine in front of us.

Hedda   For want of a scrap book – yes.

Leonard   You remember all those wild things I confessed to? Things that no one else knew – my drunkenness, my true parentage, all my sordid assignations with women – what I wanted to do with them, what I did. You had some sort of power over me that made me bare my soul, to confess.

Hedda   I had power over you?

Leonard   You always delved deeper. Questioning, scrutinising every answer so I revealed more and more . . .

Hedda   You answered all my questions freely.

Leonard   Because you were so utterly beguiling in the way you interrogated me.

How could you ask me such intimate questions? Shameless!

Hedda   Why did you answer them?

Leonard   I thought they were asked out of love – that you were trying to cleanse me of my sins – to make me a better man.

It was love!

Hedda   No. Not the sort of love you mean.

Leonard   What then?

Hedda   I was a young girl of seventeen and I wanted to understand a man's world.

Leonard   I was your guide and that was it?

Hedda   You were like Lord Shiva. You defied order and lived in ecstatic truth – untamed and magnificent with fire in your eyes. You danced past obstacles as if the world couldn't hold you. And I wanted it. Why should only men burn so brightly? Why are they the only ones allowed to consume life whole?

Leonard   You and I are cut from the same cloth. Same identity, same secrets and passions. We are bound to each other and could have taken on the world.

Why did you break with me?

Hedda   We were friends! And you tried to turn it into something serious.

Leonard   You couldn't face the truth.

Hedda   Shame on you, Lenny! How could you think of wronging your friend?

Leonard   For me it was love. Why didn't you just shoot me?

Hedda   I was seventeen and I was terrified of scandal. My father taught me that.

Leonard   You were a coward at heart.

Hedda   I still am – a terrible coward.

Beat.

Hedda's *mood cools after this admission.*

Hedda   But it was a lucky thing for you. And now you have consoled yourself so beautifully at the Humphries'.

Leonard   I know what Alice told you.

Hedda   And perhaps you have confided to her something about us?

Leonard.   Not a word. She is too stupid to understand anything of that sort.

Hedda   Stupid?

Leonard   She is stupid about that sort of thing.

Hedda   And I am a coward.

Hedda *comes up very close to* **Leonard**.

Hedda   But now I will confess something to you.

Leonard   Well?

Hedda   The fact that I dared not shoot you down . . .

Leonard   Yes!

Hedda   That wasn't my worst cowardice that evening.

Leonard   It wasn't knowledge that you wanted – it was life!

Hedda *gets scared and pulls back.* **Leonard** *is hurt.*

Hedda   Take care! Don't presume you know me.

Shona *enters. She notices* **Hedda** *and* **Leonard**'s *closeness and is not pleased.*

Shona   Mrs Humphries is here.

Hedda   Thank you, Shona. Do show her in.

Hedda *closes the album with a bang and calls out.*

Hedda   Ah, at last! My darling Alice, come in.

Alice *enters.*

Hedda   My sweet Alice – you can't think how I have been longing for you!

Alice *gives* **Hedda** *her hand.* **Leonard** *and* **Alice** *greet each other with a silent nod.*

Hedda   The three of us are going to have such a cosy evening together.

Alice   Won't George be joining us?

Hedda   No, he's going out soon to John's place for a party.

Alice (*to* **Leonard**)   Not you?

Leonard   No.

Hedda   Leonard stays with us.

Alice *is about to seat herself at* **Leonard**'s *side.*

Alice   How nice it is here!

Hedda   Not there! You come over here like a good girl. I want to be in the middle.

Alice   As you wish.

They all swap seats.

Leonard   Isn't she lovely to sit and look at?

Hedda   Only to look at?

Leonard   The two of us are very close. We trust each other completely.

Alice   I'm so happy, Hedda! He says I have inspired him too.

Hedda   Ah! He says that does he?

Leonard   She has bravery which leads to action, Mrs Tesman.

Alice   Me – brave?

Leonard   Immense courage – where friendship is concerned.

Hedda   Courage! If only I had that.

Leonard   Yes?

Beat.

Hedda *changes her tone suddenly.*

Hedda   But now, my dearest Alice, you really must let me serve you with a glass of cold punch.

Alice   No thank you. I never drink.

Hedda (*cold determination*)   Well, you then, Leonard.

Leonard   Thank you, I don't either.

Alice   No, he doesn't.

Hedda (*to* **Leonard**)   But suppose I want you to?

Leonard   Makes no difference.

Hedda (*laughing*)   Then I have no power over you?

Leonard   Not where that's concerned.

Hedda   Seriously, I think you ought to – for your own sake.

Alice   Hedda!

Hedda   Or rather, because of other people.

Leonard   Other people?

Hedda   People might think that you're afraid to drink with them.

Alice   Please, Hedda!

Leonard   People can think what they like.

Alice   Who cares what others think?

Hedda   I saw it very clearly in John's face a moment ago. That contemptuous smile of his when you didn't dare join him in there.

Leonard   I wanted to stay and chat with you here . . . and with Alice.

Alice   That was quite understandable, Hedda.

Hedda   I noticed the way he smiled and glanced at my husband when you were afraid that your resolve would fail if you went along to his wretched little party.

Leonard   You think I'm afraid.

Hedda   Not me. But that was how John understood it.

Leonard   Let him.

Hedda   So you are not going with them?

Leonard   I am staying here with you and Alice.

Alice   Yes, Hedda, of course. He must stay with us. That was the plan.

Hedda   Firm as a rock! A man of unshaken principles! As a man should be! (*Turns to* **Alice** *and caresses her.*) Now, isn't that what I said when you came to us this morning in such a state of panic.

Leonard   What?

Alice (*terrified*)   Hedda – oh, Hedda!

Hedda   See! Not the slightest reason for you to be so terribly anxious about him. Now, the three of us can relax and have a nice evening!

Leonard   Mrs Tesman, what is this all about?

Alice   What are you saying? What are you doing?

Hedda   Don't get excited!

Leonard   So Alice, you were anxious – on my account!

Alice   Oh, Hedda – how could you?

Leonard   So much for your belief in me.

Alice   My dearest friend, you must let me explain . . .

Leonard *takes one of the glasses of punch, raises it to his lips.*

Leonard   Your health, Alice!

He empties the glass, puts it down, and takes the second.

Alice   Hedda. You did this deliberately!

Hedda   Don't be silly. I didn't do anything.

Leonard   Here's to your health too, Mrs Tesman. Thanks for the truth. Hurrah for the truth!

Leonard *empties the glass and is about to re-fill it.*

Hedda *lays her hand on his arm.*

Hedda   No more for now. Remember you still have an invitation to John's party.

Alice   No, no, no!

Hedda   Hush! They can hear you.

Leonard (*putting down the glass*)   Alice, tell me the truth.

Alice   Yes.

Leonard   Does your husband know that you followed me?

Alice   Why are you behaving like this?

Leonard   Was it arranged between you and him that you were to come to town and spy on me? Perhaps it was your old husband himself that made you come? No doubt he wanted my help in his writing! Or was it that he missed me at the card table?

Alice (*softly, in agony*)   Lenny!

Leonard (*seizes a glass and is on the point of filling it*)   Here's a glass for the old writer too!

Hedda   No more. Remember, you have to read your script to George.

Leonard *suddenly stops himself and looks embarrassed.*

Leonard (*calmly, putting down the glass*)   I'm sorry, Alice. I've made a complete fool of myself. Talking like that – don't be angry with me. I'll show you – I'll show you both and the others that however worthless I may have been in the past, I've found my feet, with your help, Alice.

Alice   Thank goodness

George *and* **Brack** *enter.*

Brack   Hedda, it's time for us to be off.

Leonard (*rising*)   Yes, John.

Alice (*softly and imploringly*)   Oh, Lenny, don't!

Hedda (*pinching her arm*)   They can hear you!

Alice (*with a suppressed shriek*)   Ow!

Leonard (*to* **Brack**)   You were kind enough to invite me.

Brack   So you're coming after all?

Leonard   Yes, many thanks.

Brack   I couldn't be more pleased.

Leonard *picks up the manuscript.*

Leonard (*to* **George**)   I really would like to talk to you about my film.

Perhaps read you some extracts?

George   Excellent – I want to hear the whole script!

Hedda dear, how is Alice to get home?

Hedda   I'm sure we can manage it – somehow.

Leonard   I'll come again and fetch her. At ten or thereabouts, Mrs Tesman?

Will that do?

Hedda   Perfect.

George   But you must not expect me as early as that,
Hedda.

Hedda   Stay out as long as you like.

Alice   Leonard, I will stay here until you return.

Brack   Well, gents – shall we hit the party? Here's hoping
it's a lively one.

George   Goodbye, goodbye, ladies.

Leonard   About ten o'clock, then.

Brack, **Leonard**, *and* **George** *exit.*

Alice *is wandering restlessly about the room whilst* **Hedda** *seems
elated.*

Alice   Hedda, Hedda – how is this all going to end?

Hedda   At ten o'clock, he will be here.

Alice   I hope you're right.

Hedda   You may doubt him, Alice, but I have absolute faith
in him. I can see him already – with fire in his eyes – flushed,
fearless and true to himself.

Alice   You are so strange.

Hedda   You'll see, Alice. He will be himself again, a free
man for the rest of his days.

Alice   What are you up to, Hedda!

Hedda   I want, for once in my life to have control over a
man's destiny.

Alice   You have control.

Hedda   I don't.

Alice   Not over your husband's?

Hedda   Do you think that's worth the trouble? You have no idea how trapped I am in this world – whilst you – you just do whatever the hell you want. I think I will burn your hair after all.

Hedda *grabs* **Alice***'s hair in her hands.*

Alice   Let me go! Let me go! You're frightening me, Hedda!

Shona *enters. she looks appalled at* **Hedda***'s behaviour.*

Shona   *Memsahib* – supper is laid out in the dining room.

Hedda   We're coming.

Alice   No, I want to go home.

Hedda *pushes* **Alice** *almost by force to the doorway.* **Alice** *looks terrified.*

Hedda   Nonsense! You silly little thing. First we will have tea.

And then at ten o'clock, Leonard will be here – with fire in his eyes.

Hedda *drags the frightened* **Alice** *out and they exit together.* **Shona** *follows them.*

Act III

DAY 2. Early – around 7am.

Alice, *wrapped in a large shawl, and* **Hedda**, *fully dressed, lie sleeping.*

Shona *enters carrying a blanket. She approaches* **Hedda** *and looks at her for a moment before tucking the blanket lovingly around her.*

The stove is lit – but burning low.

Alice *wakes with a start. She looks around her – stares at her wristwatch.*

Alice   Oh God, no, no . . .

She sees **Shona**.

Alice   Has anyone come?

Shona   Yes, a girl just brought this letter.

Alice   A letter! Give it to me!

Shona   No, it's for the master, Ma'am.

Alice   Oh.

Shona   It was Miss Tesman's servant. I'll put it here.

Alice   Yes, do.

Shona (*putting down the letter*)   It's been a long night.

Alice   It'll be daylight soon.

Shona   It is daylight already, Ma'am.

Alice   Broad daylight – and no one back yet!

Shona   I guessed how this would turn out.

Alice   Did you?

Shona   Yes, I know all about Leonard Webb. He's a scoundrel.

Alice   No! You're wrong about him!

Shona   Am I? I knew him in India, when my mistress was a teenager. He used to come every day to the General's house – trying to win her over with his big ideas and his fancy talk.

Alice   Leonard knew Hedda?

Shona   He does a wonderful, tortured artist act. Full of fantastical ideas.

Always playing the victim and the women fall for it every time. Poor fools.

Alice   And Hedda?

Shona   The General put a stop to it. Thank goodness. Wherever that man goes, he brings a violent storm with him.

Alice   You shouldn't talk about people like that.

Shona   I'm a woman of the world. You should take this as a warning. Drunks are incapable of loving. The only thing they love is alcohol.

Alice   Don't speak so loud! You will wake Hedda.

Shona (*looks towards* **Hedda**)   Let her sleep, poor thing.

Shona *exits.* **Hedda** *stirs.*

Hedda   What time is it, Alice?

Alice (*looks at her watch*)   It's past seven.

Hedda   Where's Leonard?

Alice   He didn't come – no one came back at all.

Hedda   And we sat up watching and waiting here 'til four in the morning.

Alice   Waiting and waiting . . .

Hedda   We might have saved ourselves the trouble.

Alice   Did you get a little sleep?

Hedda   Oh yes – I slept quite well. Did you?

Alice   I couldn't sleep a wink. Kept imagining the worst . . .

Hedda   There, there! Nothing to be so worried about.

I know exactly what happened.

Alice   Do you?

Hedda   They had a party at John Brack's – and it went on until very late.

Alice   That is clear enough. But all the same . . .

Hedda   And then, you see, George and Leonard didn't want to crawl in and wake us in the middle of the night. Probably worse for wear and too ashamed to show their faces. Went to George's aunts' and slept there. Apparently, they've kept his old room ready for him – done up especially with all his old toys.

Alice   I don't think they're there because a letter just came for George from his aunt.

Hedda (*looks at the address*)   That's his Aunt Julia's handwriting – in which case they stayed at Brack's. And Leonard is sitting, reading his manuscript to George with fire in his eyes.

Alice   Oh, Hedda, you are just saying things you don't believe yourself.

Hedda   You really have no faith, Alice.

Alice   I'm losing hope. Hedda, you knew Leonard when you were young?

Hedda   What?

Alice   The maid said you were teenage friends.

Hedda   Did she? He used to come to the house and visit the General.

Leonard and I were never friends.

Alice   She said that . .

Hedda   Never mind what the maid said. She's a busybody and likes to stir trouble.

Alice   Why do you keep her on then?

Hedda   Habit I suppose and she's rather wonderful at doing my hair and make up.

You look dead tired, Alice.

Alice   I am.

Hedda   Do what I tell you. Go and lie down in my bed for a while.

Alice   I won't be able to sleep.

Hedda   I am sure you will.

Alice   But your husband is bound to come soon now, and I'll want to know immediately.

Hedda   I'll make sure to let you know when he comes.

Alice   Promise, Hedda?

Hedda   Yes, you can depend on me. You just go up and have a sleep in the meantime.

Alice   Thanks. I'll try.

Alice *exits.*

Hedda *draws back the curtains. The broad daylight streams into the room.* **Shona** *enters with a make-up bag, creams and brushes and starts to expertly make her up.*

Shona   My guess is, he's drunk in a ditch somewhere after boring some poor woman of the night with stories of his glorious intellect.

Hedda   You could hold a grudge for centuries.

Shona   You nearly fell for him.

Hedda   I nearly shot him. And why did you tell Alice that I knew him when I was young?

Shona   After all these years, he's still playing the same games and he's got his teeth into this poor, sweet girl. I wanted to warn her off.

Hedda   She's hardly a girl and if I'm right, she probably wrote that script for him.

Shona   Hold firm. Don't let him in again. He'll ruin you. He'll tell everyone your secret and then where will we be? There. Perfect.

Hedda   It's a new world out there and I want to be part of it. Things can change.

Shona   New world perhaps but nothing will change.

Hedda   Ma . . .

Shona   Shhh . . . Alice is only upstairs. I fought hard to make sure your father gave you his name. You want to throw that all back in my face?

Hedda   Why are you so determined to make me live a lie?

Shona   Because I remember what happened before you were the great Hollywood darling – Hedda Gabler – the way people treated you.

Hedda   Don't you feel any shame, scurrying around like a skivvy? You should be free. India's free now.

Shona   But the English are the same. They came, they had their fun and we are what was left behind. In the eyes of the white world, you are marked by the shame of their desire, so we take from them, we take everything we can get.

You reveal who – what you really are, and your work will be disparaged, and they'll never let you make another film again in your life. Worse, the press will hound and abuse you for the rest of your life. Don't imagine for a second that the Indians will come to your rescue. They hate us even more.

You're shivering.

Hedda   I wish I could just be myself.

Shona   You'd never be a leading lady again. They wouldn't allow it. You're shivering.

Hedda   It's so cold.

Shona *exits.* **Hedda** *sits as if holding her breath, unsure of what the day will bring. After a short pause, she stokes the fire and* **George** *enters, still wearing his coat and hat.*

Hedda   Good morning.

George (*startled*)   Hedda! Good heavens – you're up early.

Hedda   Don't speak so loud. Alice is resting in my room.

George   Has she been here all night?

George *takes off his hat and coat.*

Hedda   Yes, since no one came to see her home.

George   Ah . . .

Hedda   Did you enjoy yourselves at Brack's?

George   Have you been worrying about me?

Hedda   No, not at all. I was just asking if you enjoyed yourself.

George   Yes. Especially the beginning of the evening; Lenny read his entire script out to us. All hand-written in his tiny scrawly hand . . .

Hedda   Did he have fire in his eyes?

George   Not exactly, but . . . oh, Hedda, you can't conceive what a film it's going to be! I believe it is one of the most remarkable scripts that has ever been written.

Hedda   What is it about?

George   It's set in India at the end of the Raj and it's about a woman who passes for English but who has Indian blood in her. The film is almost entirely from her point of view and it's heart breaking. She tries to come back to England and pretends that she is English but when her secret comes out, she is outcast from society. Her friends, even her husband rejects her. I confess, Hedda. When he had finished reading – an ugly feeling came over me. I felt utterly jealous of Lenny for having it in him to write such a wonderful script. So much passion and depth.

Hedda *tries to hide her alarm.*

George   And then how pitiful that he – with all his gifts – should be beyond saving, after all. He just can't control himself.

Hedda   What happened?

George   It all descended into drunken shouting, singing and dancing. I joined in a bit but Lenny was the loudest. He made a long rambling speech in honour of the woman who had inspired him in his work.

Hedda   Did he name her?

George   No! But I can't help thinking he meant Alice.

Hedda   She's not Eurasian.

George   Half-caste? Alice? No . . . Lenny is though. He confessed that his mother was an Indian dancer and his father – Anglo Indian – worked in the Indian railways! Fancy that? Leonard's got a bit of the tar brush himself.

Hedda *is affected by* **George**'s *words.*

Hedda   Where did you part from him?

George   On the way home, we left in a group and Brack came with us to get a breath of fresh air. But then we decided to take Lenny home because he was completely legless.

Hedda   I daresay.

George   But now comes the extraordinary bit, Hedda, or, I should rather say, the sad bit of it. I am almost ashamed, for Lenny's sake, to tell you.

Hedda   Do go on.

George   As we were getting near his lodgings, I dropped behind the others a little, for a minute or two and then, as I hurried to catch up – what do you think I found by the roadside – virtually in the gutter?

Hedda   What?

George   Don't say anything to anyone, Hedda. Promise me, for Leonard's sake.

George *pulls out a script, from his coat pocket.*

I found this.

Hedda   Isn't that the script he had with him yesterday?

George   Yes, it's his entire, precious, irreplaceable film script! He lost it and didn't even realise.

Hedda   But why didn't you just give it back to him there and then?

George   I didn't dare – honestly – the state he was in.

Hedda   Do the others know that you had found it?

George   That would be so embarrassing to him. There were people there from the industry. They would think him such an idiot. I couldn't show him up.

Hedda   So no one knows that you have Leonard's script?

George   No. And no one must know it.

Hedda   And then what happened?

George   He gave us the slip with a couple of friends and disappeared.

Hedda   They must have seen him home then.

George   I hope so. And Brack left us and went back to his place.

Hedda   So what have you been doing with yourself since?

George   I and some of the others went home with one of the party, a jolly fellow, and took our morning coffee with him; or perhaps I should rather call it our night coffee? But now, when I have rested a little, and given Lenny, poor fellow, time to sleep it off, I must take this back to him.

Hedda   No – don't give it to him! Not yet. Let me read it first.

George   No, my dearest, Hedda, I couldn't.

Hedda   Why not. All you men got to hear the script. I want to read it too.

George   But can you imagine the state he'll be in when he wakes and realises he hasn't got his script? He hasn't made a copy. He told me so himself.

Hedda   Surely it can be reproduced – rewritten?

George   No, I don't think that would be possible. It's a matter of inspiration you see.

Hedda   I suppose you're right.

By the way – there's a letter for you from your aunt.

She hands him the letter.

It came early this morning.

George *lays the script down, opens the letter, runs his eye through it.*

George   Oh, Hedda – she says poor Aunt Rina is dying!

Hedda   That was to be expected.

George   She writes that if I want to see her again, I must be quick. I'll run in to them at once. Hedda, can't you come with me?

Hedda (*recoils*)   No. I can't deal with illness or death.

George   That's a shame . . . My hat . . . My overcoat . . .

Shona *enters as* **George** *scrambles to put his coat back on.*

George   I do hope I'm not going to be too late.

Shona   John Brack is at the door and wishes to know if he may come in.

George   At this moment! No, I really can't see him now.

Hedda   But I can. (*To* **Shona**.) Ask John to come in.

Shona *exits.*

Hedda (*quickly, whispering*)   The script, George!

Hedda *snatches it up.*

George   Yes, give it to me!

Hedda   No, no, I will keep it till you come back.

Hedda *hides the script.* **George** *watches* **Hedda**, *worried, as* **John Brack** *enters from the hall.*

Hedda   You're an early bird.

Brack   Aren't I? (*To* **George**.) You off out?

George   Yes, I must rush off – poor Aunt Rina is lying at death's door.

Brack   Oh dear. Then on no account let me hold you up.

George   Yes, I must really rush. Goodbye! Goodbye!

George *exits quickly.*

Hedda   Poor George. Still, you seem to have had a fun night.

Brack   I haven't even had time to change my clothes.

Hedda   Not you, either?

Brack   What has George been telling you of the night's adventures?

Hedda   Some dull story. Only that they went and had coffee somewhere or other. Tell me your version of last night. I'm sure it's much more exciting.

Brack   I had special reasons for keeping an eye on my guests – last night.

Hedda   I assume you mean Leonard?

Brack   He read out his script.

Hedda   And?

Brack   It is urgent, lyrical and unrelenting.

Hedda   So you liked it?

Brack   Not just liked – I was transfixed. It's a love letter and a battle cry in equal measure. He says it's unfinished but it's perfect as it is. However, do you know where he and a few others ended up spending the rest of the night?

Hedda   If it is not too shocking, tell me.

Brack   Bottom line, he ended up in a particular private club in Mayfair. The lady who runs the club was giving a party with a select circle of her admirers and her friends.

Hedda   'A lady who runs the club'? You mean a madame?

Brack   A very classy stripper. She's a mighty huntress of men. Apparently Leonard was one of her ardent supporters in his heyday.

Hedda   And how did all this end?

Brack   Far from amicably, it appears. After a most tender reunion, they seem to have come to blows.

Hedda   Leonard and she?

Brack   He accused her or her friends of having robbed him. He declared that his notebook had been stolen and a few other things as well. In fact, he seems to have kicked up a hornet's nest.

Hedda   And what was the result?

Brack   A fight in which both the ladies and the gentlemen were involved.

Fortunately, the police arrived in the end.

Hedda   Extraordinary.

Brack   It will prove a costly episode for Leonard – fool. He was completely drunk.

Hedda   Oh dear.

Brack   He shattered a glass and carved up a constable's face – slashed his cheek, Hedda – blood everywhere! They arrested Leonard and dragged him off to the station with the others.

Hedda   How do you know all this?

Brack   From the police themselves. And I spoke to Leonard in the cell – managed to get bail for him but it's an ugly affair and he will be charged.

Hedda   No fire in his eyes?

Brack   Fire?

Hedda   So he had a bit of a fall from his high principles. This sort of thing happens all the time within our circle.

Brack   This went beyond the normal bar room brawl. It obviously can't be a matter of complete indifference to me if it comes out at the trial that before this incident, he had been my guest at my place.

Hedda   Trial? Can't you use your influence – stop the matter going to court?

Brack   My influence doesn't quite stretch that far. As a friend of the family, I thought that it was my duty to supply you and George with a full account of his nocturnal exploits.

Hedda   Why?

Brack   Because I've got a hunch, he's going to be using you as cover.

Hedda   Oh, how can you think such a thing!

Brack   Good heavens, Hedda, we have eyes in our head. Mark my words that Alice isn't in any hurry to pack her bags and to go back to her husband.

Hedda   Even if there is anything between them, there must be plenty of other places where they could meet.

Brack   I daresay Leonard won't find a respectable door left open to him.

Hedda   And you think I should close my doors to him too?

Brack   Yes. I admit it would be very unpleasant to me if this man was a constant visitor here, if he were to insinuate himself into . . .

Hedda   . . . the triangle?

Brack   Precisely. I should find myself homeless.

Hedda   So you want to be the only cock in the yard? That is your plan?

Brack   Yes, that is my plan. And for that I will fight with all the means at my command.

Hedda   All that brilliant writing will go to waste?

Brack   His script is dynamite, but he hasn't changed – his behaviour last night was disgraceful. He can't hold his drink;

his mouth runs away with him and he's violent – downright nasty. He's just not the right sort.

Hedda   And what is the right sort?

Brack   To add oil to the fire, last night Leonard revealed that he's a mongrel.

His mother was an Indian dancer or something. Did you know?

Hedda   Of course not. But why should that make any difference?

Brack   Doesn't matter to me, not personally. If anything, I think the man's past lends his work grit – texture you can't fake. But this industry? You know how it is. No one'll touch him now. Not here, and certainly not in the States. Still . . . I could buy the script, throw him a cheque, thank him kindly, get another director.

Hedda   An English director?

Brack   Yes, and you could still play the leading lady.

Hedda   A Eurasian?

Brack   Why not? We could use make up – darken you up a little – you'd be perfect. I've always thought you had rather exotic looks. Those eyes . . .

Brack *stands very close to* **Hedda**. **Hedda** *holds her ground.*

Brack   Think it over, Hedda. With me in your corner and this role, you could be the star you were born to be – all that glory, right back where it belongs. I know you want it. So go on – tell me your terms.

Hedda   You really are a most dangerous man.

Brack   Do you think so?

Hedda   I am beginning to. And I am relieved that you have no sort of power over me.

Brack   Well, well, Mrs Hedda – perhaps you are right there. If I had, who knows what I might be capable of?

Hedda   That sounds almost like a threat.

Brack   Oh, not at all! The triangle, you know, ought, if possible, to be spontaneously constructed.

Brack *pulls away.*

Brack   I'd better be getting back to town. I mean to get my hands on Leonard's script.

Hedda   Are you going through the garden?

Brack   Yes, it's a short cut for me.

Hedda   And then it is a back way, too.

Brack   Quite so. I have no objection to back ways – it can be quite exciting.

Hedda   When there is shooting practice going on, you mean?

Brack   Oh, people don't shoot their tame farmyard poultry.

Hedda   Not when they have only one cock in the yard.

Brack *exits.*

Hedda, *who has become quite serious, stands for a moment looking out. Eventually she takes* **Leonard**'s *script out of the hiding place and is on the point of looking through its contents.* **Shona** *is heard speaking loudly in the hall.*

Shona (*off*)   No! No! You can't go in in that state!

Hedda *turns and listens. Then she hastily hides the packet.*

Leonard *storms in confused and agitated.*

Leonard (*looking towards the hall*)   And I tell you I must and will come in!

Shona *stands behind him – furious.*

Shona   Mr Webb just barged past me, Memsahib.

Hedda   It's alright, Shona. Thank you. You may leave us.

Shona   But, Memsahib . . .

Hedda (*firm*)   You may leave us.

Shona *exits, reluctantly, shooting a warning look at* **Hedda**. *On seeing* **Hedda**, **Leonard** *at once regains his self-control but he looks distraught and unkempt.*

Hedda   You're a little late to come and fetch Alice.

Leonard   Or rather early to call on you. My apologies.

I suppose George isn't up yet.

Hedda   No.

Leonard   When did he come home?

Hedda   Pretty late.

Leonard   Did he tell you anything?

Hedda   Yes, I gather you had a very jolly evening.

Leonard   Nothing more?

Alice *enters.*

Alice   Lenny! At last!

Leonard   Yes, at last. And too late!

Alice   What is too late?

Leonard   Everything is too late now. I'm finished.

Alice   Don't say that!

Leonard   Wait until you've heard what I'm going to tell you.

Hedda   Perhaps you would prefer to talk alone? I will leave you.

Hedda *turns to leave.*

Leonard   No, stay. I beg you.

Alice   I don't need to hear anything about it. Honestly.

Leonard   It is not last night's adventures that I want to talk about.

Alice   What is it then?

Leonard   Just this – Alice, it's over between us.

Alice   No!

Hedda (*involuntarily*)   I knew it!

Leonard   You can't help me anymore, Alice.

Alice   What are you saying?

Leonard   You heard me.

Alice   I can still help you. We can still work together.

Leonard   I won't be working any more.

Alice   Then what will I do with my life?

Leonard   You must try to live your life as if you had never known me.

Alice   I can't do that!

Leonard   You must go home.

Alice   Never! Wherever you are, that's where I want to be! I won't be packed off like this. I will stay here! I will be with you when you make the film.

Hedda   Yes, your film, Leonard.

Leonard   Mine and Alice's film.

Alice   And that is why I have a right to be with you when it comes out! I will see you praised and honoured again. And the joy – I want to share the success with you. To show how proud I am . . .

Leonard   Stop. Please stop. Alice, our film will never happen.

Hedda   Ah!

Alice   Why?

Leonard   Can never.

Alice   Lenny – what have you done with the script?

Hedda   Yes, the script?

Alice   Where is it?

Leonard   I have torn it into a thousand pieces.

Alice   Oh no, no!

Hedda   But that's not . . .

Leonard   It's true.

Alice   Oh God – oh God, Hedda. Torn his own work to pieces!

Leonard   I have torn my own life to pieces. So, I might as well tear up my life's work too.

Alice   And you did this last night?

Leonard   Yes. Tore it into a thousand pieces – and scattered the pages on the Thames – far out. Let the scraps of paper drift with the wind and the tides into the sea. And after a while, they'll . . . they will sink deeper and deeper as I will, Alice.

Alice   Why would you do such a thing?

Leonard *can't find any words.*

Alice   Why, Lenny – so cruel – why?

Leonard   You cannot save me again, Alice. You brought me back to life for a moment and I almost believed I could change. But I can't.

Alice *looks at* **Hedda** *who turns away.* **Alice** *sobs a little but quickly gathers herself.*

Alice   I want you to know, Lenny – that what you've done to the script . . . for the rest of my life it'll be for me as though you've killed a child.

Leonard   You're right – I've murdered a child.

Hedda (*quietly*)   Ah, the child –

Alice   How could you? It was my child too.

Alice *collects her things and turns to leave.*

Hedda   Alice, where are you going?

Alice   I don't know.

Alice *exits.*

Hedda   You're not going to see her home?

Leonard   Would you have people see her walking with me? It would destroy her reputation.

Hedda   I don't know what else went on last night, but is it so utterly irretrievable?

Leonard   It isn't just last night – it will go on happening. I know myself well enough. But the curse of it is, I don't want to start all that again. She has broken my spirit and taken my courage. I've no fight left to drink myself fearless and spit in the eyes of the world.

Hedda   So that pretty little fool did have her fingers in a man's destiny.

Leonard   Let me tell you the truth, Hedda, but promise me you won't ever tell Alice.

Hedda   What?

Leonard.   The script – I didn't tear it to pieces or throw it in the river, but it's gone.

Alice said I murdered a child, but killing your child is not the worst thing a father can do, is it?

Hedda   You're making no sense, Lenny.

Leonard   Imagine, Hedda, that a man crawls home at dawn to his child's mother after a night of debauchery, and says, 'Listen, I've been drinking and whoring all night and I took our child out with me and now I've lost them. No idea where they are who has our child now.'

Hedda   It's just a script.

Leonard   Alice's soul was in that script. I can never look her in the face again.

Hedda   You made another fatal mistake last night. You revealed your Indian mother to John.

Leonard   So, you *did* hear what happened? Should have seen their faces when I told them, Hedda. They were disgusted. No one will work with me now. Even if I could rewrite the script from memory – what would be the point? People like us . . .

Hedda   People like us . . .

Leonard   Anglo Indians. Our voices silenced, our identities ridiculed . . . cowering inside our pale skins.

Hedda   And you had the audacity to write a film about me with *her*.

Leonard   How do you know what I wrote about?

Hedda   You read the whole thing out last night apparently – not to me but to George and John Brack! I cannot abide the idea of people gossiping about my identity.

Leonard   I never revealed . . .

Hedda   Do you know what this would do to my career if people found out?

You were going to drag me down with you.

Leonard   No. No! That was not my intention.

Hedda   You of all people know how hard it was to crawl my way up.

And yet you thought it was perfectly alright to fabricate a story about my life?

Leonard   You were my inspiration. You and I are outcasts in this world. Comrades! I wanted to tell our story. Why shouldn't the world hear our story?

Hedda   My life's story is not yours to tell.

Leonard   It's gone now.

I thought I had a second chance – after the war. But I'm haunted – not a day goes by it when it doesn't all come back again . . . The screaming sirens, the planes catching fire, my comrades dying, burnt alive in their cockpits. I can't sleep at night, keep thinking of all those young pilots I shot down. And to think, I fought a war for the British – the same cold-hearted colonialists who hold their pure whiteness up against my face and say I'm dirty, that I'm not good enough, my life is not worth as much as theirs.

Hedda   What are you going to do now?

Leonard   I will try to end it all – the sooner the better.

Beat.

She steps towards him

Hedda   Lenny – will you try to do it beautifully?

Leonard   Beautifully? Untamed and magnificent with fire in my eyes, as you used to imagine in the old days?

Hedda   I don't believe in that anymore. But beautifully, nevertheless.

Leonard   Give George my love.

Leonard *is on the point of going.*

Hedda   Wait a moment! I must give you a souvenir to take with you.

Hedda *fetches the pistol case, then returns to* **Leonard** *with one of the pistols.*

Leonard   *This?* This is the souvenir?

Hedda   Don't you recognise it? It was aimed at you once.

Leonard   You should have used it then.

Hedda   Take it and use it yourself.

Leonard (*puts the pistol in his breast pocket*)   Thanks!

Hedda   And beautifully, Lenny. Promise me that!

Leonard   Goodbye, Hema Gabler.

Leonard *exits.*

Hedda *listens for a moment at the door. Then she retrieves the script from its hiding place, peeps under the cover, draws a few of the sheets half out and looks at them. She holds the script to her breast for a moment and then decides.*

She opens the stove door, lifts one page and throws it into the fire. She watches it burn for a moment and then starts to feed the script page by page into the fire.

Hedda   Now I am burning your child, Alice with the golden hair! Your child and Leonard's. I am burning – I am burning your child.

The pages of the script burn.

Act IV

DAY 2. Evening. The same rooms.

Hedda *walks up to the window, lifts the curtain aside a little and looks out into the darkness deep in contemplation. Her thoughts are interrupted as* **Shona** *enters, followed by* **Julia** *dressed in mourning.*

Shona   Memsahib, Miss Tesman.

Hedda *walks towards* **Julia** *and holds out her hand.* **Shona** *exits.*

Julia   Hedda. My poor sister has found peace at last.

Hedda   Yes, George sent a message to tell me the sad news.

Julia   He promised he would. I thought, all the same here, in this house of life, I ought to bring the news of my sister's death to Hedda in person.

Hedda   That was very kind of you.

Julia   Rina should not have died now. This is not the time for Hedda's house to be a house of mourning.

Hedda *(changing the subject)*   She died peacefully, didn't she?

Julia   Her end was so calm, so beautiful. And then she had the unspeakable happiness of seeing George once more, so she was able to say goodbye to him. Isn't he back home yet?

Hedda   No. He said he might be detained. Won't you sit down?

Julia   No thank you, my dear, precious Hedda. I should like to, but I have so much to do. I must prepare my dear one for her rest as well as I can. She shall go to her grave looking her best.

Hedda   Can't I help you in any way?

Julia   Oh, you must not think of it! Hedda mustn't do that kind of thing.

Don't dwell on mournful thoughts or work now.

Hedda   One is not always mistress of one's thoughts.

Julia   Bless you. Ah yes, it is the way of the world. At home we'll be sewing a shroud, and there'll be sewing to be done here too. I think soon, but that will another kind of sewing. Thank God!

George *enters.*

Hedda   George, at last!

George   You here, Aunt Julia?

Julia   My dear boy. We shall both miss her terribly.

George   You and Aunt Rina – it was like having two mothers. And now . . .

Julia   I am still here and of course Hedda. Have you seen to those things you promised?

George   No, I'm afraid I've forgotten half of them. I'll run over to yours again tomorrow. My head is so muddled today, I just can't think straight.

Julia   Why, my dear George, you mustn't take it in this way.

George   I mustn't?

Julia   Even in your sorrow you must rejoice, as I do – rejoice that she's at peace now.

George   Oh yes, yes – Aunt Rina.

Hedda   It will be lonely for you now, Aunt Julia.

Julia   Yes. It will be. But to be honest, both Rina and I have been lonely for the past ten years. We missed our home in India so much. The banyan tree in the garden, the beautiful, scented tuberoses, the sun, the warmth of the people. And we don't have the servants – I have one maid here and she's so surly! In Bombay we had a cook, maids, a butler, a chauffeur . . . you remember our chauffeur, Gopal?

George   Dear Gopal. Always smiling.

Julia   I know. But it's hard. Rina's last words were that she wished we had never left.

George   You couldn't stay there. India is an entirely different country now. If you hadn't left, they would have run you out of town.

Julia   Breaks my heart to think we'll never go back there, never see those faces again. They almost felt like family. We thought we were coming home to England, but actually that was our true home.

Hedda *is deeply affected.*

George   Auntie, Hedda and I are your family. We'll be here for you.

Julia   I daresay I shall soon find an occupant for Rina's little room. Then I won't feel so alone. I need someone to live for and after all, there may soon be something in this house, too, to keep an old aunt busy.

Hedda   Please don't bother yourself about . . .

George   Think how happy we three could be together.

Hedda *looks horrified.*

Julia   You have plenty to talk to each other about.

Goodbye! I must go home to Rina. (*Turning at the door.*) How strange it is to think that now Rina is with me and your poor father at the same time.

Julia *exits.*

Hedda   I almost think your Aunt Rina's death affects you more than it does your Aunt Julia.

George   It's not only Aunt Rina's death. It's Lenny I'm uneasy about. I looked in at his rooms earlier this evening, intending to tell him the script was in safe keeping.

Hedda   And?

George   No one was there, but on the way home I met Alice, and she told me that he had been here early this morning.

Hedda   Yes, just after you had gone.

George   And he said that he had torn his manuscript to pieces?

Hedda   Yes, so he said.

George   Why, good heavens, he must have been completely out of his mind!

And I suppose you didn't give it back to him, Hedda?

Hedda   No, he didn't take it.

George   But you told him that we had it?

Hedda   No. Did you tell Alice?

George   I thought it best not to. But you ought to have told him.

Suppose he goes off in desperation and does himself an injury?

Hedda   Over a script?

George   It's his life's work! Let me have it, Hedda! I'll dash over to his immediately. Where's the parcel?

Hedda   I don't have it.

George   Where is it then?

Hedda   I have burnt it – every line of it.

George (*horrified*)   Burnt! Burnt Lenny's manuscript!

Hedda   Don't scream like that. Shona will hear you.

George   Burnt! Why, good God! No, no, no! It's impossible!

Hedda   It's true, all the same.

George   Do you know what you've done, Hedda? It's unlawful appropriation of lost property.

Hedda   I advise you not to speak of it to anyone else.

George   But how could you do anything so terrible? What put it into your head? What possessed you?

Hedda   I did it for your sake, George – darling. This morning when you told me about what he had read to you; you said that you envied his work.

George   I didn't mean that literally.

Hedda   I could not bear the idea that anyone should throw you into the shade.

George   Hedda! Oh, is this true?

But – but – I never knew you to show your affection like that before.

Hedda   Now you know – darling, I may as well tell you that – at this moment . . . (*Impatiently breaking off.*) No, no; you can ask Aunt Julia. She'll explain it to you.

George   I think I understand you. Hedda! Do you really mean it!

Hedda   Stop shouting. Shona might hear.

George (*laughing/over the moon*)   Why, how absurd you are, Hedda. It's only Shona! I'll go out and tell Shona myself.

Hedda   Oh, it is killing me, it's killing me, all this!

George   What is, Hedda?

Hedda   All this grotesque nonsense, George.

George   Do you see anything grotesque in my being overjoyed at the news! But after all, perhaps I had better not say anything to Shona.

I should tell Auntie first. And then that you have begun to call me darling too! Fancy that! Oh, Auntie will be so happy, so happy!

Hedda   When she hears that I have burnt Leonard's manuscript – for your sake?

George   No, of course nobody must know about that business . . . But that you love me so much, Hedda – Auntie must really share my joy in that!

(*Looks uneasy and downcast again.*) And yet the script – the script! Dear God! It is terrible to think what will become of poor Lenny now.

Shona *enters.*

Shona   Memsahib, Mrs Humphries is here to see you.

Alice *enters.*

Alice (*agitated*)   Hedda, do forgive my coming again.

Hedda   What is the matter, Alice?

Alice   I went to Leonard's lodgings and asked for him there.

George   And?

Alice   His landlady said he hadn't been home since yesterday afternoon.

Then, as I was leaving, I heard people talking about Lenny outside in the street.

Hedda   What were they gossiping about?

Alice   I couldn't make out anything clearly . . . . the thing is, they stopped talking when they saw me, and I didn't dare to ask I am so afraid that some accident has happened to Lenny . . .

George (*moving about uneasily*)   We must hope, we must hope that you misunderstood them, Alice.

Hedda   What exactly did you hear?

Alice   Something about the hospital or . . .

Hedda   No, surely not!

Alice   I was so frightened!

George   Maybe I should go and make some inquiries?

Hedda   No, no, don't get mixed up in this affair.

Shona *enters.*

Shona   Mr Brack is here to see you.

John Brack *enters as* **Shona** *exits.*

George   John . . .

Brack   It was imperative I should see you this evening.

George   You have heard the news about Aunt Rina?

Brack   My condolences, George. And I'm afraid, there's more bad news.

George   What's happened?

Brack   Leonard has been taken to the hospital.

Alice (*shrieks*)   Oh God! Oh God!

George   Dying?

Hedda   So quickly then.

Alice (*wailing*)   And we parted in anger, Hedda!

Hedda   Alice, Alice – come now.

Alice   I must go to him! I must see him alive!

Brack   It won't be any use, dear Lady.

Alice   At least tell me what happened to him.

George   Did he do it himself?

Hedda   Yes, I am sure he has.

Brack (*keeping his eyes fixed on* **Hedda**)   Unfortunately, you have guessed quite correctly, Hedda.

Alice   Oh, how horrible!

George   A suicide attempt?

Hedda   Shot himself.

Brack   Rightly guessed again, Hedda

Alice   When did it happen, Mr Brack?

Brack   This afternoon, between five and six.

George   But, good Lord, where did he do it?

Brack   I suppose at his lodgings. He had shot himself in the chest.

Alice   How awful!

Hedda (*to* **Brack**)   Are you sure – in the chest?

Brack   Yes, as I said.

Hedda   Not in the temple?

Brack   In the chest.

Hedda   Well, well, the heart is a good place, too.

Brack   How do you mean?

Hedda (*evasively*)   Oh, nothing – nothing.

George   And the wound is dangerous?

Brack   Absolutely fatal. The end must have come by this time.

Alice   Yes, yes, I feel it. The end! The end!

George   How did you find this all out, John?

Brack   Through one of the police. A man I had some business with.

Hedda   There's beauty in this.

Alice   How can you talk of beauty in such an act!

Hedda   Leonard has himself made up his account with life. He has had the courage to do what had to be done.

Alice   No, we must not believe that was how it happened! It must have been a moment of madness.

George   Done in despair!

Hedda   That he did not. I am certain of that.

Alice   Yes, yes! Just as when he tore up our script.

Brack   Has he torn that up?

Alice   Yes, last night.

George (*whispers softly*)   Oh, Hedda, we shall never get clear of this business. (*To everyone.*) To think of Lenny going out of the world in this way! And not leaving behind him the film that would have made his name!

Alice   I wish we could rewrite it for him.

George   Did he make notes? Have another draft?

Alice   No. No!

Alice *searches in her bag.*

But I scribbled things down . . . here . . . from the ideas, the character descriptions, scene outlines, notes on our discussions . . .

Hedda (*a step forward*)   Ah!

George   Oh, do let me see them!

Alice *hands* **George** *a bundle of papers.*

Alice   But they are in such a mess, all mixed up together.

George.   We could work on this, get it straight. We could make something out of them! Perhaps if we put our heads together. I can remember a lot of detail from last night.

Alice   We could try.

George   We must! I will dedicate my life to this task.

Hedda   You, George? Your life?

George   Yes, or rather all the time I can spare. My own film must wait in the meantime. Hedda – you understand? I owe this to Lenny's memory. We both do.

Hedda   Perhaps. But wouldn't that be stealing his story?

George   It's his story of course – but he's no longer here, so we must tell it for him.

Alice   I will do the best I can.

George   Come. I can't rest until we have looked through the notes. Where shall we sit? Here? No, in there, in the front room – the light is better. Do excuse me, John. Come with me, Alice.

George *and* **Alice** *exit.*

Hedda   What a sense of freedom it gives one, this act of Leonard's.

Brack   It certainly is a release for him.

Hedda   I mean for me. It gives me a sense of release, in knowing that there can be such a thing in the world as bravery in action. An act of spontaneous beauty.

Brack (*looking hard at her*)   Leonard was more to you than perhaps you are willing to admit to yourself.

Hedda   You're such a jealous man, John.

Leonard lived his life fearlessly. And then in this last great act, he had the courage to take leave of his life early, on his terms. Beautifully.

Brack   I'm afraid I must deprive you of your romantic fantasy.

Hedda   What do you mean?

Brack   Leonard did not shoot himself – voluntarily. The thing did not happen exactly as I said.

Hedda   What did you leave out?

Brack   I covered up a few facts for Alice's sake. In the first place, he is already dead.

Hedda   At the hospital?

Brack   Yes, I was there by his side as he took his last breaths.

Hedda   What else have you concealed?

Brack   The thing didn't happen at his lodgings.

Hedda   What difference does that make?

Brack   Leonard was found shot in a certain boudoir in Mayfair.

Hedda *makes a motion as if to rise but sinks back again.*

Brack   He went there, they said, to demand the return of something which they had taken from him. Talked wildly about a lost child.

Hedda   And he was found there?

Brack   Yes. With a pistol which had gone off in his pocket. The shot wounded him fatally.

Hedda   In the chest, yes?

Brack   No, it hit him here.

He points at his groin.

It was an accident.

Hedda (*looks up at him with an expression of loathing*)   So sordid! Everything I touch seems to become so sordid.

Brack   There is one more sordid point, Hedda, another disagreeable feature in the affair. The pistol he carried.

Hedda   Well? What of it?

Brack   He must have stolen it.

Hedda   Stolen it! That's not true. Why do you think that?

Brack   Any other explanation is unthinkable, or ought to be.

Hedda   I see.

Brack   Leonard was here this morning, wasn't he?

Hedda   Yes.

Brack   Were you alone with him?

Hedda   Part of the time.

Brack   And you left the room while he was here?

Hedda   No.

Brack   Think it over. Didn't you go out of the room for a moment?

Hedda   Yes, perhaps just a moment. Why are you questioning me like this?

Brack   Because this is exactly what the police will be asking you. I saw the pistol they found in Leonard's pocket, and I recognised it at once from yesterday.

Hedda   Have you got it?

Brack   No, the police have it.

Hedda   What will the police do with it?

Brack   See if they can find the owner.

Hedda   Do you think they will succeed?

Brack (*bends over her and whispers*)   No, Hedda Gabler – not so long as I hold my tongue.

Hedda   And if you don't?

Brack   You could always say he stole it.

Hedda   I'd rather die.

Brack.   People often say that – but they never do it.

Hedda (*looks at him, frightened*)   What if the pistol wasn't stolen, and the owner is discovered? What then?

Brack   A court case. Witnesses brought to the stand. In a word, scandal – which you seem to have a deadly fear of.

Hedda   But I have nothing to do with all this repulsive business.

Brack   No. But you will have to answer the question: why did you give Leonard the pistol? And what conclusions will people draw from the fact that you did give it to him?

Hedda *is distraught.*

Brack   And another thing. I know the real story of Hema Gabler.

Hedda *does not react.*

Brack   Born, in Calcutta to an Indian woman, the low caste servant of General Gabler, brought up in India. Sent to private school where she was ridiculed by her classmates for being a 'coon'. Had to leave school and be educated at home. But General Gabler taught her how to ride a horse, how to shoot and most of all he taught her entitlement.

Hedda   Lies.

Brack   Not lies. Leonard told me everything right there in the hospital, an hour before he died. Oh, and actually, he wrote it in his film script – the one that he tore up after seeing you. May I continue?

Hedda *seems stunned.*

Brack   Leonard was a half-breed too, used to drop by the Gabler place for tea with young Hema. She hung on his every word as he talked about his passions, his big dreams. When her father died, she was left with nothing. The

General left her high and dry. But Leonard . . . Leonard gave her something to hold onto. Something to believe in.

Hedda   Stop.

Brack   Hema Gabler – had elocution lessons and because she passed for white and was extraordinarily beautiful, she determined to enter the world of cinema. So, off went Hema with her Indian mother – I mean – maid – here to London where she worked in the bars before catching the eye of an elderly famous director. And so Hedda Gabler became who she is today. But no one knows that she isn't pure bred. They don't know that she's a mongrel – half-caste.

I wonder what the film industry would do if they found out? There are censorship codes in Hollywood and here, of course. You would not be seen as having – how did that reviewer from your last film put it? 'Hedda Gabler does not have apple pie appeal.'

Hedda *is devastated.*

Brack   That's it, isn't it? The real reason why you retired. You were worried that they were on to you; that your career would be finished.

Fortunately, there is no danger, so long as I say nothing.

Hedda   So I am in your power. You have me at your beck and call, from this time forward.

Brack (*whispers softly*)   Dearest Hedda – believe me – I shall not abuse my advantage.

Hedda   In your power none the less. At the mercy of your will and your demands. A slave, a slave then! No – never!

Brack   One generally gets used to the inevitable.

Hedda *looks* **Brack** *in the eye.*

Hedda   Does one?

George *enters followed by* **Alice.**

Hedda   How are you getting on, George?

George   Goodness, this is going to be a lot of work but I think we could cobble something together.

Alice   It will be hard to straighten out.

Brack   If you could quickly write a script from Alice's notes, then you can direct it, George, and we have a film to shoot. I'll get the ball rolling.

George (*excited*)   We must manage it. Lenny had such a passion for this film, and I can see why. It's an extraordinarily heart-breaking story and the main character – a wonderful part for you Hedda, if only you would come out of retirement.

Hedda *strokes her hands softly through* **Alice's** *hair.*

Hedda   Doesn't it seem strange to you, Alice? Here you are sitting with George, just as you used to sit with Leonard?

Alice   If I could only inspire your husband too.

Hedda   Oh, that will come in time.

George   Yes, do you know, Hedda, I really do feel inspired.

But you stay here with John.

Hedda   Is there nothing I can do to help you both?

George   No, not a thing . . . (*Turning his head.*) Would you be so kind as to keep Hedda company, John?

Brack   With the very greatest of pleasure.

George   I'll tell you what, Alice, you should take the empty room at Auntie's, and then I will come over in the evenings, and we can sit and work there.

Hedda   But what am I supposed to do?

George   I'm sure John will look in now and then, even though I am out.

Brack Every blessed evening, with all the pleasure in life, Hedda! We shall have a very happy time together – you and I.

Hedda Yes, that's what you're looking forward to, isn't it? You, as the only cock in the yard.

Hedda *pulls out her pistol and plays with it in her hand.*

George Oh, now she is playing with those pistols again.

Hedda *points the pistol at her head and holds it there smiling.*

Shona *enters and watches horrified.*

Alice Hedda! What are you doing?

George Hedda, please!

Shona Darling, child – no! Don't. Please . . .

Hedda *looks across at* **Shona** *in triumph.*

Hedda (*to* **Shona**) Finally, I'm being brave.

Brack Put that thing away.

Hedda *turns the pistol around and instead points it directly at* **Brack**.

Everyone No! Hedda! Stop!

Gunshot as **Brack** *falls to the floor. Everyone screams/shouts and rushes to* **Brack**'s *body.* **Hedda** *turns the pistol around, points it to her head. A second gunshot rings out.*

Blackout.

www.ingramcontent.com/pod-product-compliance
Lightning Source LLC
Chambersburg PA
CBHW041923090426
42741CB00020B/3462